The
Smart Growth
Manual

Andres Duany, FAIA, CNU (Miami, FL) is a founding principal of Duany Plater-Zyberk & Company (DPZ). DPZ is a leader of the New Urbanism, an international movement that seeks to end suburban sprawl and urban disinvestment. Since 1980, DPZ has designed over 300 new towns, regional plans, and community revitalization projects. Duany is cofounder of the Congress for New Urbanism and the recipient of several honorary doctorates and awards, including the National Building Museum's Vincent J. Scully Prize and the Richard H. Driehaus Prize. With Elizabeth Plater-Zyberk and Jeff Speck, he is co-author of *Suburban Nation: The Rise of Sprawl and the Decline of the American Dream.*

Jeff Speck, AICP, CNU, LEED-AP, Hon. ASLA (Washington, DC) spent 10 years as director of town planning at DPZ, where he led or managed more than 40 of the firm's projects. Subsequent to the publication of *Suburban Nation*, he was appointed director of design at the National Endowment for the Arts, where he created the Governors' Institute on Community Design, a program that brings smart growth techniques to state leadership. After four years at the Endowment, he founded Speck & Associates, a design consultancy serving public officials and the real estate industry. He is a contributing editor to *Metropolis* magazine.

Mike Lydon, CNU (New York, NY) is an urban planner, writer, and livable streets activist. Before founding The Street Plans Collaborative, an urban planning firm specializing in alternative transportation and the public realm, he worked for DPZ, the Massachusetts Bicycle Coalition, and Smart Growth Vermont. He is currently a Next American City Urban Vanguard and serves as a board member for the Miami Bicycle Coalition.

Cataloging-in-Publication Data is on file with the Library of Congress.

McGraw-Hill books are available at special quantity discounts to use as premiums and sales promotions, or for use in corporate training programs. To contact a representative please e-mail us at bulksales@mcgraw-hill.com.

Smart Growth Manual

1 2 3 4 5 6 7 8 9 0 DOC/DOC 0 1 4 3 2 1 0 9

ISBN 978- 0-07-137675-4
MHID 0-07-137675-5

The pages within this book were printed on acid-free paper containing 100% postconsumer fiber.

Sponsoring Editor
Joy Bramble Oehlkers
Acquisitions Coordinator
Michael Mulcahy
Editorial Supervisor
David E. Fogarty
Copy Editor
Patti Scott
Proofreader
Beatrice Ruberto
Production Supervisor
Richard C. Ruzycka
Art Director, Cover
Jeff Weeks
Cover Illustration
Eusebio Azcue / DPZ

This publication was supported by C.A.T.S.: The Center for Applied Transect Studies. www.transect.org

The
Smart Growth
Manual

Andres Duany
Jeff Speck
with Mike Lydon

New York • Chicago • San Francisco
Lisbon • London • Madrid • Mexico City
Milan • New Delhi • San Juan
Seoul • Singapore • Sydney • Toronto

Contents

Introduction

The Region

The Neighborhood

The Street

The Building

Appendix

Index

Introduction

What Is This Manual For?

This manual is intended to be a central resource for those who intend to put smart growth into practice and to assess the work of those who purport to do so. While there are many good publications on this topic, we have not found any single one that attempts this role. It is presumptuous of us to claim this ground, and we expect as many critics as supporters of this effort. But the issues are too important to be left to those with less experience building new places and fixing old ones.

Some people will find that this manual says too little. Its goal was not to catalog all aspects of good development practice, but rather to emphasize those that need attention. This explains why it is a single book and not a multi-volume encyclopedia. Most of the items in this manual would benefit from a longer discussion than is offered. The quick argument of each point—which threatens to make light of some important issues—results from the desire for both a wide scope and a narrow spine; so does the limited amount of design theory and supporting documentation. Above all, this publication is meant to be handy. It was written with a realistic attitude about how few books are actually read, particularly by those people busy building things. We would rather see these pages criticized for their brevity than avoided for their length.

On the other hand, there are some artistically inclined spirits who will find that this manual says far too much. Its high level of specificity is the product of a long experience that has led us to value the known over the speculative. Simply put, we believe that new places should be designed in the manner of existing places that work. Humans have been building settlements for a long time, and there is much to be known about their success and failure. The most spectacular failures of the recent past were attempts to replace time-tested models with unprecedented inventions.

While we sometimes wish it were otherwise, planning is a technique more than an art. As in medicine or the law, its evolution should be constant but must occur atop a foundation of knowledge collected through the centuries. Any design can be considered clever simply by being novel, but it cannot be trusted until it has been shown to produce positive outcomes.

For that reason, this manual bases smart growth upon the traditional mixed-use neighborhood. It was the abandonment of this model in favor of novelties that led to the current crises—ecological, economic, and social—that make the smart growth campaign necessary. There may be other, more creative ways to reorganize our national landscape, and many of these may be sustainable, but the neighborhood is the only one that has proved itself so, ten thousand times over.

The central importance of the neighborhood structure can be deduced by studying Miami-Dade County, the crucible in which many of this manual's ideas were forged. The Miami metropolitan area achieved very early almost all the features that have come to be identified with smart growth: a unified regional government and single school district; an elevated rail system supplemented by a pervasive bus network and a downtown people mover; an extremely dense settlement pattern; and a tightly drawn urban growth boundary—one of the nation's first. Yet, it is a place in which almost everyone drives to almost every destination. This outcome is due, plain and simple, to the absence of neighborhood structure. Without tight networks of walkable streets centered on mixed-use neighborhood centers, the residents of Miami will not walk to or from transit, however nice the weather.

Given glamorous newer developments such as green building and low-impact stormwater facilities, it is easy to forget that the old, dependable neighborhood structure is the very heart of smart growth. Its details are missing from most books on the subject, and they are not sufficiently emphasized in the LEED standards. Restoring the centrality of the neighborhood structure to the American environmental movement would be the most important contribution of this manual.

Also unconventional is this manual's emphasis on the details of physical design, particularly at the scale of the streetscape and the individual building. These issues are rarely addressed with specificity in the smart growth discussion. They, too, deserve attention, because all scales are connected. For example, window mullions increase visual privacy for interiors, allowing dwellings to be closer together. This increases density and creates more spatially intimate streets that encourage walking. Walking supports transit and reduces vehicle miles traveled (VMT). In turn, reduced VMT lowers carbon-based emissions and therefore slows climate change. To the infinitely complex human—particularly the demanding North American version—even mullions matter.

While many people are talking about smart growth, only a few are implementing it. But, after more than 25 years of efforts, it is now possible to reach conclusions about what works. The techniques described here are known to make a difference. They are offered with the confidence that, if disseminated widely, they can dramatically improve the state of our environment and the quality of our lives.

This manual is not about the idiocy of suburban sprawl or the superiority of smart growth. That subject is well covered by a library of publications—some of them our own—that first hit the shelves almost as soon as sprawl hit the ground. If you are looking for arguments against the current pattern of development, books such as *Suburban Nation* and *The Long Emergency* are readily available. It is our assumption that, if you are reading this manual, you do not need convincing. Rather, you need resources and practical explanations about what to do.

It has been a struggle to relearn the full range of techniques surrounding good neighborhood design, but the last decades have witnessed great progress toward this essential goal. We hope that this manual gets us there sooner.

What Is Smart Growth?

That is a question we asked ourselves years ago, when the term began to gain currency. Is that the kind of design that we have been practicing at our firm? Some of us didn't like the term. One colleague, a marketing expert, told us not to use it. "It's mean. It implies that everyone else is dumb." For others, that was its best feature.

Ultimately, the choice was not ours to make. Championed first by Governor Parris Glendening of Maryland, then by the Environmental Protection Agency, next by a growing collection of organizations bearing its name, smart growth stuck. The challenge then became to attach the proper techniques to the name.

This manual began a decade ago as our attempt to do just that, but the task was harder than we expected. After reviewing the literature, conferring with experts, and consolidating our experience, we found the first draft to be immediately out of date. The technical situation was evolving too quickly, projects were still being implemented, and research was advancing beyond our capacity to track it. New Urbanism, green building, agricultural reform, the Climate Project, and other initiatives were just beginning to coalesce. We put the manual on hold and listened.

What has emerged from these primordial rumblings is a sort of unified field theory. It is clear that the form of our communities is the fundamental determinant of so many things that matter, and that a half-century of, yes, dumb growth has put our nation and our species in a truly precarious position. The movement against suburban sprawl, which began principally as an aesthetic and social critique, is now working in the service of science. Climatologists link sprawl to the global warming crisis. Economists link sprawl to our dependence on foreign oil. Environmentalists link sprawl to declines in air and water quality. Public health officials link sprawl to an epidemic of obesity and diabetes, not to mention 40,000 car-related deaths a year. Smart growth has become, as Mayor John Norquist said of the New Urbanism, "the convenient remedy for the inconvenient truth."

It is now clear that many current social, economic, environmental, and physiological ills are direct outcomes of the way we have built our communities since World War II. Single-use zoning, massive road construction, and urban disinvestment have turned a nation of ecologically sustainable neighborhoods into a collection of far-flung monocultures, connected only by the prosthetic device of the automobile. We learn from biology that monocultures cannot thrive and that hypermobility is a sign of impending extinction. Yet most states and municipalities still promote policies that favor single-use zoning and free-flowing traffic rather than mixed-use, pedestrian-oriented urbanism.

To understand our national building culture, it is useful to imagine a gigantic ship headed toward treacherous shores. The captain has spotted the danger and ordered the engine room to reverse course. But the ship advances, driven by its momentum. In our situation, the captain represents the intellectual leadership of the development industry: the American Planning Association, the Urban Land Institute, the Congress for the New Urbanism, and the many government agencies that have embraced smart growth. The ship's momentum stands for all the entrenched laws, policies, practices, and special interests that have accumulated over six decades of sprawl. At the time of this writing, this momentum has been slowed only by the mortgage-backed financial crash—arguably another outcome of sprawl. But it will pick up again, and when it does, our future depends on the smart growth model being firmly in place. The current respite will perhaps be viewed by historians as fortunate. It gives us time to think. We trust that, during this time of questioning, our method of designing communities will attract as much critical scrutiny as our method of financing them.

Indeed, in monitoring the crises surrounding climate change, energy dependence, public health, decaying infrastructure, and financial instability, we are reminded that all five are the result of sprawl and thus can find solutions only in smart growth.

So, if smart growth is what we need now, what is it? We know that it is the opposite of automobile-based suburban development. But it is possible to be much more precise. In creating this manual, we reviewed the publications of more than 30 different organizations that either are focused exclusively on smart growth or have addressed it in their agendas. They approach the topic variously. As one might imagine, the smart growth publications of the National Association of Homebuilders are not identical to those of the Sierra Club. However, there is scarce contradiction between the actual principles put forth by these diverse groups. The differences amount to what issues each organization has chosen to ignore. These exclusions reflect the specialized concerns of each group.

Because most of these disagreements take the form of omissions, it seems possible to create a more complete, less politicized set of principles simply by being resolutely inclusive. Such an attempt can be found on the pages that follow.

The Region

The Region

Because growth is inevitable, it must be shaped into the most intelligent possible form through regional plans that are based upon the model of the mixed-use neighborhood and organized around the logic of the urban-to-rural transect. In these plans, which are prepared publicly, growth is directed toward existing infrastructure, affordable housing and potentially undesirable land uses are distributed equitably, and productive farmland as well as natural assets are protected. For regional planning to be truly effective, property taxes should be shared among municipalities, and government should be organized to correspond with the physical structure of settlement. Municipalities promoting smart growth should demonstrate its principles through their own building efforts, while reforming their codes to allow the expansion of choice that smart growth represents. Finally, cities without adequate water resources should not grow, and cities that are becoming less populous should have plans that creatively engage that reality.

Inevitable Growth

Replace *No Growth* with *Good Growth*.

Portland, OR: By directing growth to downtown locations, Portland has become one of America's most vital cities.

The very term *smart growth* implies that development can be positive, and, until the advent of sprawl, this was the common understanding. Today, the poor quality of our built environment has convinced many people that good growth is not possible, and that the only option is to stop development entirely. Such an approach is untenable, as the population of this country is expected to grow by 30 million over the next 20 years. *No-growth* campaigns, even when successful, tend to last one or two political terms at most, and often serve as an excuse to avoid planning altogether. When such policies are eventually reversed due to housing shortages, growth quickly resumes in its worst form. The first step of effective long-term planning is to admit that growth will occur, and the second step is to focus on its quality.

A Regional Plan

Think globally, act locally, but plan regionally.

The Louisiana Speaks Regional Plan designates transportation corridors, intended growth sectors, and protected open space.

Regional planning is essential, for it alone operates at the true scale of people's lives. Planning a single town or city is not enough, because working, shopping, recreation, education, and other daily activities routinely take people across municipal lines. Without regional-scale determinants such as natural corridors, transit systems, and designated urban centers, even the best local planning may contribute to sprawl. However, effective regional planning is rare, because few municipalities are organized to coordinate administratively at a scale encompassing the entire metropolitan area. Such planning is therefore ideally commissioned at the next level up, by the government body that includes the full metropolis—often a county or state. Failing direct government sponsorship, this planning can be managed effectively by organizations that have been chartered to address a regional issue such as transportation, air quality, or water management.

Community Involvement

Seek community consensus for all plans.

Memphis, TN: A hands-on workshop led by the National Charrette
Institute allows citizens to help shape their community.

While it is easier to plan behind closed doors, only a dictator can turn private plans into public reality. Thanks to the relatively recent democratization of the development process, the question is no longer whether the public will participate, but when and how. Wise governments and developers understand that the time to seek community participation is at the outset, using public opinion to help guide the project rather than to derail it at a later date. Experience shows that, when presented with the facts, a truly representative community group will usually advocate for smart growth, whose popularity has been demonstrated nationwide through visual preference surveys and polls. The challenge for planners is to thoroughly communicate the issues to a representative set of citizens, rather than meeting only with those self-selecting and single-issue groups that tend to dominate the discussion. This requires a range of communication tools, including charrettes, newspaper supplements, and real-time web posting.

1.4 The Transect

Plan according to the logic of a rural-to-urban transect.

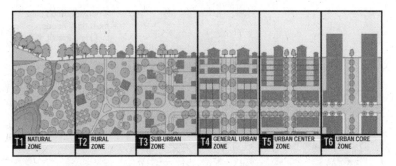

| T1 NATURAL ZONE | T2 RURAL ZONE | T3 SUB-URBAN ZONE | T4 GENERAL URBAN ZONE | T5 URBAN CENTER ZONE | T6 URBAN CORE ZONE |

A transect provides meaningful lifestyle choices
within a smart growth framework.

The transect is a concept drawn from ecology. It is a progression through a sequence of habitats, such as from wetland to upland to foothill. Ecologists use the transect to describe how each habitat supports symbiotic sets of mineral conditions, microclimate, flora, and fauna. The rural-to-urban transect extends this classification system to include a sequence of human habitats of increasing density and complexity, from the rural hinterland to the urban core. Design at every scale should correspond to the logic of transition from the natural edge to the man-made center. As described in the pages ahead, transportation, planting, buildings, setbacks, and all the myriad details of the human habitat vary across the transect. What matters is not whether the transition between transect zones is made gradually or abruptly— Fifth Avenue can line Central Park—but rather whether the details of each transect zone are internally consistent and therefore mutually supportive. This logic of place coordinates the techniques that lead to sustainable urban environments, which in turn provide for the variety of lifestyles that Americans desire and are, in most places, legally entitled to.

1.5 The Neighborhood

Plan in increments of complete neighborhoods.

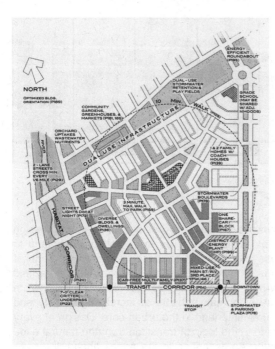

A neighborhood puts most daily needs, including transit, within a short walk.

With the exception of regional-scale corridors and special-use districts, growth should be organized as neighborhoods. The term *neighborhood* has the specific technical meaning of being compact, walkable, diverse, and connected. It is *compact*—as dense as the market will allow—in order not to waste land, and it is typically no larger than a half-mile across. It is *walkable* in that this size corresponds to a five-minute walk from edge to center and that all its streets are pedestrian-friendly. It is *diverse* in that it can provide the full range of daily needs, including shopping, workplace, and housing for all ages, incomes, and living arrangements. Finally, it is *connected* in that it is seamlessly integrated into transit, roadway, and bicycle networks. The neighborhood is not an innovation; it has been the fundamental increment of human settlement throughout history, interrupted only by the 60-year aberration that we now call suburban sprawl. Traditional villages, towns, and cities across the centuries and across cultures are all assembled from this same basic building block. The smart growth of a region can be measured by the strength of its neighborhood structure.

1.6 Growth Priorities

Direct investment to smart growth priority areas.

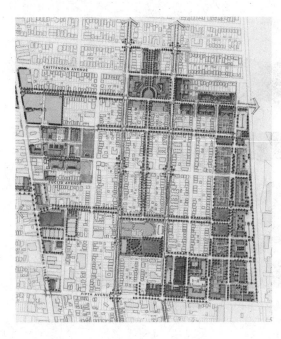

Columbus, OH: The Weinland Park master plan directs public improvements to urban-infill areas to encourage their development.

Smart growth directs both public infrastructure funding and private development where they will have the greatest economic, environmental, and social benefit. This approach requires a clear prioritization of growth alternatives, from smartest to "dumbest," as follows:

1. Urban revitalization
2. Urban infill
3. Urban extension
4. Suburban retrofit
5. Suburban extension
6. New neighborhoods on existing infrastructure
7. New neighborhoods requiring new infrastructure
8. New neighborhoods in environmentally sensitive areas

Once this hierarchy is established as policy and designated on a regional map, governments can attract development to the high-priority areas through a range of incentives. Maryland Governor Parris Glendening described his state's program this way: "We told communities that they're still free to sprawl—we're just not going to subsidize them anymore."

Affordable Housing

Require every area to accommodate subsidized dwellings.

Cincinnati, OH: The City West HOPE VI neighborhood provides a range of affordable and market-rate housing near the urban core.

A metropolitan area cannot function effectively unless every municipality provides its fair share of affordable housing. The burdens of concentrated poverty are best overcome by distributing lower-cost housing throughout the region. Again, Maryland provides a useful example: Montgomery County has required all large developments to include 10 percent of affordable dwellings, thus creating 10,000 such units over 20 years. This program, applied nationwide, could potentially shelter the 5 million American households currently spending more than one-half of their incomes on housing. Such housing should be located principally in places where proximity to transit provides ready access to jobs and services without the added financial burden of automobile ownership.

Distribution of LULUs

Allocate locally undesirable land uses fairly and logically.

Michigan City, IN: Power plants and other unwanted neighbors are typically located where they encounter the least political resistance.

Locally undesirable land uses (LULUs) can be allocated only at the regional scale. These range from the dramatic (power plants and landfills) to the mundane (large, traffic-ridden hospitals and high schools). Halfway houses, homeless shelters, and other such facilities are also hotly contested LULUs which everyone agrees are necessary but wants deposited in someone else's neighborhood. As a result, they are often dumped in disadvantaged communities where they meet the weakest opposition, or relegated far away to the urban fringes where they isolate people who do not drive. Objective regional criteria can be developed to site LULUs properly—according to existing patterns of land use and transportation, and with a concern for social justice.

Food Security

Ensure food supply by retaining farmland.

Montgomery County, MD: Thanks to the Piedmont Environmental Council, over 180,000 acres of farmland have been placed under permanent conservation easement.

The typical American meal travels 1500 miles from farm to plate, consuming an extraordinary amount of energy in shipping and refrigeration. As the costs of energy climb, long-distance food sourcing will become increasingly untenable, and metropolitan areas without an agricultural hinterland will have difficulty feeding themselves within their means. Cities that hope to thrive in the long run must secure and enlarge their productive farm belts. This is best accomplished at the state level, where ballot measures have recently demonstrated a public willingness to fund the preservation of open space.

Shared Wealth

Allocate property tax revenue equitably across the region.

Minneapolis, MN: The Fiscal Disparities Act of 1971 established tax revenue sharing across the seven-county Minneapolis–St. Paul metropolitan region.

While considered somewhat radical, property tax sharing is an essential tool for metropolitan stability. Many of the decisions that generate suburban sprawl result from competition for tax base. Every revenue-challenged jurisdiction wants to land big-box retailers, deluxe McMansions, and manufacturing plants, and will thus open up rural areas to get them. If property taxes were shared regionally, local governments would no longer implement exclusionary zoning to escape tax-negative housing, and the urban core would lose fewer residents due to underfunded police and schools. As Minnesota's Myron Orfield puts it, "sharing property taxes makes regional land-use policies possible."

LILD: tax location   *tax centrality for mixed use*
                            tax isolation for domus

Scale of Governance

Coordinate government and neighborhood structure.

SUBSIDIARITY

New York, NY: The Far West 10th Block Association is just one of several in Greenwich Village that provide self-governance at an appropriately local scale.

While regional planning suffers because few governments exist at the scale of the region, local planning suffers because governance rarely operates at the scale of the neighborhood or the block. Just as there is a hierarchy of physical structure—from the metropolis to the neighborhood to the block—there is a need for a corresponding hierarchy of governance. The frustration that some citizens feel toward their municipal administration arises when these government entities do not correspond to the scale of the people's concerns. The great popularity of "private government"—the suburban homeowners' association—derives from people's desire for direct accountability from their representatives. The sense of common destiny with one's neighbors has engendered many block associations in older neighborhoods. Without growing, local governments should reconstitute themselves to match the physical structure of their communities. Some noteworthy successes are the block associations of Manhattan and the NETs (Neighborhood Enhancement Teams) of Miami.

Coordinating Policy

Avoid dumb-growth locations for government facilities.

Islip, NY: Beautiful but in the wrong place, Richard Meier's Federal Building sits isolated alongside a highway, rather than contributing activity and jobs to an existing urban core.

Governments at all levels should determine if their policies unintentionally promote suburban sprawl. At the federal level, two such practices have been identified. One is Fannie Mae's policy of making loan guarantees only to single-use projects, which deters the construction of mixed-use buildings and neighborhoods. Another is the tendency to relocate facilities such as courthouses and post offices from urban centers to new sites on the suburban fringe. Congressman Earl Blumenauer of Oregon has proposed legislation allowing downtowns to retain these important buildings and the jobs they provide. A similar effort in Rhode Island preserved downtown state office buildings that were slated to be decanted to the suburbs. At the level of municipal government, a common dumb-growth investment is the consolidated big-box school, which induces leapfrog sprawl as the housing follows.

Legalizing Smart Growth

Introduce smart growth as a way of expanding choice.

Windermere, FL: When this town needed a "traffic solution," it invested in making its downtown more pedestrian- and bicycle-friendly.

Suburban sprawl must be recognized as the default development pattern. While the past 15 years have witnessed a new thinking in the planning profession, the evidence suggests that too little has changed in reality. We can blame this situation on institutionalized business practices and rear-view-mirror marketing, but the principal cause is that in most places smart growth is technically illegal. Despite the stated policies of so many official reports and comprehensive plans, most existing codes and standards effectively outlaw the construction of compact, diverse, walkable, and connected communities. A politically realistic approach to make the necessary changes would focus less on outlawing sprawl and more on removing the impediments that make smart growth impossible. To be palatable, policies must not limit choice, but expand it to include the possibility of living in neighborhoods again.

The Limits of Water

Build only where water resources are plentiful.

Lake Mead, NV: Thirty miles southeast of Las Vegas,
the reservoir is now at one-half of its original capacity.

Some issues are so large in scale and potentially so devastating that they require policy at the national level. One of these is the problem of dwindling aquifers. This is a meta-regional issue that has pitted Nevada against Colorado, and Georgia against Alabama and Florida. Only the federal government can mediate these conflicts, but playing referee in contests over limited resources is not enough. Regions that are unable to meet their projected water needs should not be granted the federal subsidies that spur growth—from highway funds to industrial grants. Water subsidies enable most of the unsustainable sprawl in the Sunbelt. Local and state governments that support this future disaster can be checked only by the authority that exists at the scale of rivers and aquifers. Federal law must move beyond negotiating water disputes to curtailing the growth of untenable regions.

1.15 The Shrinking City

Design the controlled contraction of certain cities.

Detroit, MI: A victim of failed urban policy, the Motor City
has lost one-half its population since the 1950s.

With more than one-half of the world's population now living in urban
areas, it may come as a surprise that for every two American urban
cores that are growing, three are shrinking. In the United States alone, 59
cities with a population of 100,000 or more have lost at least 10 percent
of their inhabitants since 1950. For these, smart growth addresses not a
better way to expand, but a better way to contract. Concentrating infrastructure and services in those neighborhoods with better prospects
and encouraging disinvested areas to revert to agricultural or otherwise
productive open space are strategies that should be considered and
proactively implemented. After 30 years of industrial decline, depopu-
lation, and failed redevelopment strategies, Youngstown, Ohio, has
accepted that it is unlikely to re-attain its peak population of 250,000.
Instead, the city's award-winning 2010 Plan seeks to stabilize its population at 80,000, diversify the job base, and use incentives to entice
residents to relocate to its more viable neighborhoods.

The Region

This chapter outlines a simple 10-step process for preparing a regional plan. While this technique may require modification to reflect local circumstances, it is a protocol within which to consider all the aspects involved in an organized and interrelated way.

Map the Greenprint

Identify the region's cumulative natural resources.

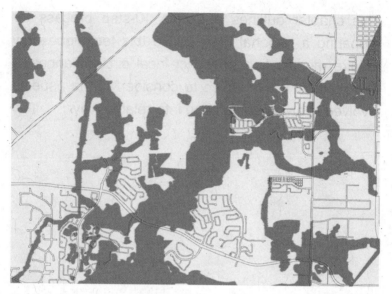

Hillsborough County, FL: This regional plan
begins by mapping the region's Greenprint.

Championed by the National Lands Trust, the Greenprint is a method
for mapping an area's natural resources to guide growth. As described
in the publication *Growing Greener*, the Community Resource Inventory
lists nine elements to be mapped:

1. Wetlands and their buffers
2. Floodways and floodplains
3. Moderate and steep slopes
4. Aquifer recharge areas
5. Woodlands
6. Productive farmland
7. Significant wildlife habitats
8. Historic, archeological, and cultural features
9. Scenic viewsheds from public roads

Unlike the Rural Preserve described next, the Greenprint does not
have the force of law, but it has value as an ideal to be considered in
planning decisions.

Map the Rural Preserve

Identify the land truly protected from development.

The regional plan next maps the areas within the
Greenprint that are legally protected.

An essential step in preserving open space is to determine what
is truly protected. The Rural Preserve consists of those portions of
the Greenprint (Point 2.1) that are prohibited by law or contract from
future development. These protected lands establish the core open-
space resource that is to be expanded over time. The map typically
demonstrates how little of the region—even within the Greenprint—is
actually safe from sprawl. It serves to alert all concerned. As
stated by the Urban Land Institute, "smart growth recognizes
the intrinsic community, economic, and environmental value of open
spaces in all communities." This understanding is shared by the public
at large: in 2007, voters approved 34 of 55 state conservation ballot
measures, making available $1.4 billion in new funding.

Map the Rural Reserve

Identify the additional land that should be protected.

The regional plan next identifies the areas of the Greenprint that are outside of the Rural Preserve. This striped zone is designated as Rural Reserve.

The Rural Reserve supplements the Rural Preserve to fulfill the Greenprint for the region. A first step in creating the Rural Reserve is to review critically the Greenprint already completed. Most of its features should be included in the Reserve, but some, such as moderate slopes, may not be reasonably defensible and may need to be left out. Next, the open-space structure of the Rural Reserve should be judiciously supplemented to create a continuous system of natural corridors. Once mapped, the Rural Reserve clearly indicates the region's highest-priority areas for open-space protection. All future efforts for land preservation—whether ballot measures, purchases by benevolent organizations, or transferred-development-rights programs (Point 2.8)—should focus on shifting land from the vulnerable Rural Reserve into the permanently protected Rural Preserve.

2.4 Map Development Priorities

Identify and rank the areas best suited for growth.

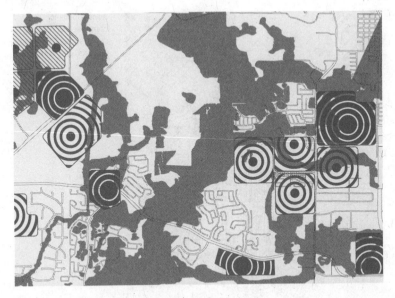

The next step of the regional plan is to designate the areas of
high, moderate, and low priority for development.

As described in Point 1.6, there is a range of growth locations from
smartest to dumbest. This hierarchy should appear as prioritized development sectors on the regional plan map. These can be described as
follows:

- Intended Growth Sectors: High-priority areas of urban infill, brown-
  field sites, and transit stops
- Controlled Growth Sectors: Moderate-priority areas of urban
  extension and suburban infill
- Restricted Growth Sectors: Low-priority areas of suburban
  extension and new development on existing infrastructure
- No-Growth Sectors: Areas of development requiring new infrastructure or in environmentally sensitive locations

Once these sectors have been mapped, governments at every level can
use incentives and coordinate policies to prioritize development (see
Points 2.8–2.10).

2.5 Map the Neighborhoods

Identify the present and potential neighborhood structure.

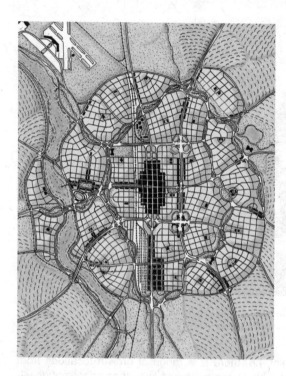

A metropolis is composed of regional centers, neighborhoods, districts, and corridors.

Urban areas consist of only four elements: regional centers, neighborhoods, districts, and corridors (see Points 2.6 and 2.7). The identification of these place types is essential to the understanding of an effective regional vision. The first step is to create a map that depicts the region's neighborhoods. Almost all urbanization prior to 1950 conformed to the neighborhood pattern of mixed-use areas within five-minute-walk pedestrian sheds. While more recent policy and practice have often undermined the original neighborhoods, it is usually not difficult to locate them. Identifying this underlying structure enables effective land-use and transportation decisions. For example, roadways within neighborhoods should rarely be widened, while those between neighborhoods may be able to support additional traffic without damaging the quality of life of the proximate residents. The mapping of a SmartCode (Point 2.10) will allocate zoning that reinforces neighborhood structure.

Map the Districts

Identify justified and unjustified single-use areas.

Clay, NY: The big-box strip is one common
type of unjustified district.

Districts are large areas dominated by a single function. They can be justified or unjustified. Justified districts include civic, medical, and college campuses; large or noxious agricultural and industrial facilities; transportation depots and terminals; and specialized entertainment zones such as Disney World. The rest are principally the unjustified districts created by unnecessary single-use zoning. They include housing subdivisions, apartment complexes, shopping centers, and business parks—developments that cause social fragmentation and traffic congestion. Unjustified districts can be rezoned by plan and coded to encourage their retrofit with additional uses. For example, some struggling malls have been transformed into mixed-use town centers, as documented in the EPA's *Greyfields to Goldfields*. Likewise, office parks may be infused with housing in place of their parking lots and useless buffers. The retrofit of sprawl by balancing and infilling unjustified suburban districts is a major objective of smart growth. A book by Ellen Dunham-Jones and June Williamson, *Retrofitting Suburbia*, presents the issue in a comprehensive manner.

Map the Corridors and Regional Centers

Identify major natural and man-made corridors.

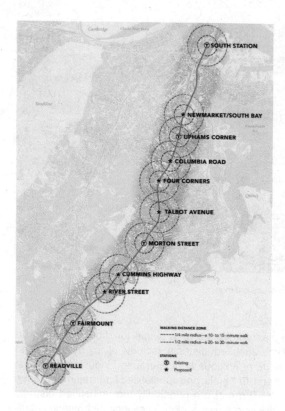

Boston, MA: This corridor plan includes mixed-income, mixed-use development around existing and proposed transit stations at regional centers.

Corridors, the fourth piece of the regional puzzle, are the linear elements that both connect and separate neighborhoods and districts. Corridors can be natural or man-made. They include waterways, greenways, rail lines, and major traffic thoroughfares. Highways and arterials are the most common corridors, especially in suburban sprawl, where many take the degraded form of commercial strip development. Known to decay periodically, these should be rezoned to gradually molt into higher intensity mixed-use regional centers served by transit. Beyond the traffic thoroughfares, rail corridors and even canals are under-used trajectories that will again be valuable in a post-petroleum economy. For this reason, they must not be vacated or converted to trails. Future corridors must be recorded so that necessary land can be acquired. The resulting corridor map should keep trajectories somewhat flexible while establishing minimum standards for each type.

2.8 Create a TDR Program

Arrange for the transfer of development rights.

Ann Arbor, MI: Sending its development rights to the urban core, the 160-acre Bur Oaks Farm joined the city's greenbelt in 2005.

Sprawl threatens the Rural Reserve because existing agricultural zoning typically permits development at a low density. Conversely, some high-priority development sectors cannot grow into real neighborhoods because their zoning prohibits density. It is necessary to move development potential out of the Rural Reserve into these high-priority development sectors. That is accomplished through the mechanism of the transferred development right (TDR). A government-run TDR program manages the sale of development potential from one site to another in support of the goals of the regional plan. Through such a program, a farmer that plans to sell his or her farm to finance the children's college tuition can instead sell off only the farm's development value while continuing to work the land. To be most effective, TDRs should be bought and sold on the open market just as real estate is.

2.9 Incentivize Smart Growth

Create a process that rewards smart growth development.

Austin, TX: The Triangle, an 859-unit mixed-use development on 22 acres, was built under the city's Smart Growth Matrix Incentive Program.

The pattern of development is as important as its location. To determine whether a project qualifies for incentives, governments should consider two factors: the priority of the project's development sector and its design's compliance with smart growth criteria. Adherence to this standard should be determined through a legally adopted form-based ordinance such as the SmartCode (Point 2.10). If a project is exemplary in both location and design, it should be placed on a fast-track approval process and considered for incentives. Municipalities that are not able to give financial help or tax relief can still offer date-certain approvals. Time, to a developer, can be as compelling as money. They should also establish an approval process that reviews conventional development only when the pipeline of smart growth applications is empty.

Adopt a Smart Growth Code

Introduce standards that allow smart growth.

The SmartCode, which makes smart growth legal at every scale, may be downloaded at www.*smartcodecentral.org*

Suburban sprawl does not just happen. In most places existing codes and public works standards have inadvertently made smart growth illegal. Governments must, at the very least, provide developers a regulatory environment in which smart growth is possible. One such set of rules is now available as freeware: the *SmartCode*. Municipalities are warned that attempting to modify a conventional suburban code into a smart growth code is difficult, if not impossible, as the two models are incompatible. But it is typically neither necessary nor politically possible to completely replace existing regulations, so the SmartCode is conceived to be introduced in parallel as an incentivized alternative. At the time of this writing, many dozens of municipalities have undertaken to implement form-based codes, including Denver, Miami, Montgomery, Sarasota, El Paso, and San Antonio.

The Region

Smart growth acknowledges the essential role that transportation plays in the shaping of communities and insists that transportation and land-use decisions be made in tandem. It seeks to regain a balance among transportation modes by encouraging walking, biking, and all types of transit, but also works to reduce the need for mobility of all sorts by promoting self-sufficient neighborhoods. These neighborhoods, to be walkable, are kept free of high-speed traffic. Proposals to expand thoroughfares are considered in light of induced traffic, in which increases in capacity result in increased congestion. Smart growth also promotes congestion pricing and car sharing to make the most of existing thoroughfares.

Transportation/Land-Use Connection

Coordinate transportation and land-use planning.

Pasadena, CA: Del Mar Station combines a light rail stop with
housing, retail, civic space, and underground parking.

Settlement patterns result from transportation systems. Historically the
five-minute-walk pedestrian shed created the neighborhood, streetcars determined the corridor structure of urban expansion, and trains
generated the nodal pattern of the early suburbs. But recently the automobile has allowed new development to spread thinly and without discipline across the landscape. The transportation/land-use connection
that is responsible for both these good and bad patterns is well known,
yet it often fails to influence planning. Municipal engineers routinely plan
new roadway extensions into areas that municipal planners are trying
to keep free of development, while planners allow new development
without considering its transportation needs. In some places, the transportation and planning departments rarely communicate. Ideally, these
two departments should be combined into a single entity. But regardless
of the departmental structure, land-use and transportation decisions
must be made simultaneously.

3.2 Multimodal Balance

Do not prioritize the car above other modes of transport.

King County, WA: Bicycle racks on buses integrate
two modes of urban transportation.

For more than half a century, transportation planning has assumed
that the private automobile is the primary means of mobility. The true
costs of a car-dependent society have now become apparent: transportation expenses rival housing costs for many American families.
Studies document the economic, social, and environmental advantages
of transit, yet federal funding favors roadways over transit by a ratio of 4
to 1. Moreover, public transit funding typically requires that all costs be
justified on the basis of current demand, which in most places has been
artificially lowered by unavailable service. To level the playing field,
transportation planning should bring transit investment into parity with
roadway subsidy, while specifying land-use patterns that contribute to
the effectiveness of all modes equitably.

Building a Transit Region

Plan transit comprehensively at the regional scale.

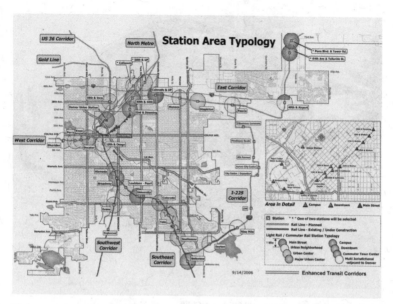

Denver, CO: FasTracks, the City and County's long-term transit plan, includes Transit Oriented Developments at future rail stops.

Transformative transit systems such as those in New York, Chicago, and Washington, D.C., were planned comprehensively for region-wide service. In contrast, metropolitan areas such as Miami have made one-line-at-a-time plans for transit, creating systems that have not affected the urban pattern. It need not be this way. Baltimore, Denver, and Seattle are currently building regional-scale networks. These investments will pay off as residents spend less and less of their income getting around. Rather than only running along available rights-of-way, new transit systems must be assigned the more difficult task of connecting employment and activity centers in support of a coordinated land-use plan. Ideally, all new growth should be located within the pedestrian sheds of current or planned public transportation stops. The most effective transportation plans, such as Portland's, mandate mixed use at planned light rail stops. Even where it is not yet planned, development should be organized in anticipation of service, with clear neighborhood centers properly spaced along a boulevard wide enough to support a light rail line or bus rapid transit lane.

Transportation Choice

Provide the contextually appropriate mode of transit.

Portland, OR: The city's streetcar system, in operation since 1999, connects commuter rail, bus transit, and a network of bikeways.

Cities have a variety of rail and bus options. In considering different systems, it is important to understand what distinguishes them. *Light rail* and *bus rapid transit* (BRT) are systems that improve efficiency by maintaining a certain distance between stops, typically a mile or more. They generally connect regional centers, which they tend to create or enliven, but provide little economic energy to areas between stops. In contrast, *streetcars* (trolleys) and *buses* move relatively slowly, stop frequently, and can enliven their entire trajectories. Streetcar rails can be laid quickly, limiting inconvenience to local businesses, and they are best placed directly in the roadway so that the vehicles are easily accessible to pedestrians. While light rail is better at providing regional mobility, investments in streetcars are better at targeting smaller urban corridors. Buses, while less expensive, do not provide the permanence or civility of streetcars and therefore are not as effective at urban revitalization. They also last a fraction as long as streetcars. Bus rapid transit is a cheaper alternative to light rail, but only effective to the extent that its path is truly expedited and protected. Too many cities' BRT systems consist only of faster-looking buses.

Transit That Works

Build transit so that it is easy to use.

Denver, CO: The Ride is a light rail system that
is well integrated into the urban fabric.

To attract ridership in communities that are already automobile-oriented,
transit must satisfy these four criteria:

- A simple trajectory: One of the reasons people prefer rail to bus
  is that the route is a line or loop, easily understood and with few
  diversions.
- Frequent headways: Most people won't look at schedules and won't
  wait more than 15 minutes, so frequent service is essential. Waiting
  can be made more bearable by the GPS-enabled time-to-arrival
  clocks which are now available.
- A dignified wait: Each transit stop must offer a safe, comfortable,
  clean, and dry place to sit, ideally with a cup of coffee and a
  newspaper available.
- Integration within urbanism: Effective transit attracts pedestrians
  more than drivers, who must shift from one vehicular mode to
  another. The path from the sidewalk to the streetcar, train, or
  bus must be direct and pleasant, not across parking lots or other
  dead zones.

The Railway System

Re-establish the missing American intercity railway.

The northeast corridor's Acela train is in high demand, thanks to its frequent, speedy, and dependable service.

The story of America's railways since the mid-twentieth century is one of neglect and abandonment. In living memory, American cities were connected by efficient rail service, and interurban lines linked suburbs and towns to their city centers. Undermined by the highway, automobile, fuel, and trucking lobbies, a once superb network has dwindled to near irrelevance. This occurred with transportation planners aware of the relative costs of alternate transport modes: even before today's oil price fluctuations, trucking was seven times more costly per ton-mile than rail shipping, and short-hop flying was twice as expensive as the train. Our need for economic efficiency, reduced dependence on foreign oil, and limited emission of greenhouse gases requires that current road-building subsidies be redistributed toward rail systems. California's recent vote to invest $10 billion in an electric bullet train is an important step. When complete, this system will take passengers from San Francisco to Los Angeles in 2.5 hours for a price of $55, and with a CO_2 reduction of 324 pounds per passenger.

3.7 Mobility and Accessibility

Plan for proximity as well as movement.

Washington, DC: Buildings combining apartments, shops, and restaurants are one reason that Logan Circle rates a 98 on the *walkscore.com* website.

Transportation planning must evolve from a focus on automobility to one on mobility—the ability to get around by a variety of means. But beyond that, mobility is less useful than *accessibility*—the ability to meet one's ordinary needs with the minimum amount of travel and cost. Why move around when destinations can be nearby? In many cases, proximity requires only that zoning allow land uses to mix at fine grain. Simply put, self-sufficient neighborhoods make mobility less important. Once again, transportation problems often have land-use solutions. Interestingly, the financial benefits of mixing uses extend well beyond transportation savings. When communities satisfy their needs for goods and services nearby, self-sufficient local economies develop, retaining wealth and saving energy to a degree that can dwarf other sustainability efforts. Known as *import replacement*, this approach should form a part of every smart growth strategy.

The Townless Highway

Protect rural thoroughfares from development.

Anywhere, USA: Strip development is the fate of most rural
highways not protected against commercial zoning.

The great failure of American planning can be found at the periphery of
every large town and city, where roads built for unimpeded long-range
transportation have become choked with local traffic. Where roads pass
through the countryside, development must be discouraged, because
it undermines the intended function of through-traffic and blights the
scenic view. When new roads are built, it is important to insist that
their construction not result in an up-zoning of roadside properties to
commercial use. Where existing roads are already zoned for commercial use, a counterforce for their protection is to establish a highway
viewshed ordinance like that enacted by Napa County in 2001.

3.9 The Highwayless Town

Protect neighborhoods from high-speed thoroughfares.

San Francisco, CA: When an earthquake damaged the Central Freeway, it was demolished and replaced by Octavia Boulevard, a neighborhood thoroughfare.

While high-volume roads can be good for commercial neighborhoods, high-speed roads destroy them. High-speed roads should either skirt neighborhoods or transform to a low-speed design as they enter them. This used to be the standard: highways became urban main streets as they entered towns. Unfortunately, this practice was not acknowledged in the postwar traffic manuals, and highways have reamed out much of America's historic urban fabric. Equally damaging, though less obvious, is the widening of state and county roads to accommodate commuting at the expense of local livability. Even while continuing to handle through traffic, roadways within neighborhoods must be designed to slow traffic to pedestrian-friendly speeds of 30 miles per hour or less. This can be done with little loss of traffic capacity.

Induced Traffic

Reject projections that ignore induced traffic.

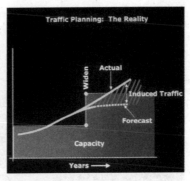

Traffic engineers routinely widen roadways based on traffic forecasts that become true only because additional traffic is attracted to the new, larger road.

Induced traffic is a phenomenon long documented by transportation experts but resolutely ignored in planning decisions. It explains the failure of new and wider roads to reduce traffic congestion: the new road capacity is absorbed by drivers who previously avoided getting on the congested road. This phenomenon was confirmed in a study covering 30 California counties between 1973 and 1990, finding that for every 10 percent increase in metropolitan roadway capacity, vehicle-miles traveled increased 9 percent within 4 years' time. As enlightened engineers put it, "trying to cure traffic congestion by adding more capacity is like trying to cure obesity by loosening your belt." If induced traffic were more fully understood, roadway infrastructure spending would be directed instead toward measures that actually do reduce congestion, such as transit, bikeways, and mixed-use zoning.

3.11 Taming the Automobile

Do not allow traffic to trump livability.

Grand Rapids, MI: The Department of Transportation has removed parking and trees from Division Street, undermining walkability in an otherwise healthy downtown.

For busy urban centers, accommodating the automobile unconditionally is a no-win game. In terms of cars circulating and parking, peak demand always outpaces supply. Successful urban areas cannot avoid having too much traffic and insufficient parking. Cities that add highways, widen roads, and demolish buildings for parking lots will only satisfy driver demand by progressively becoming undesirable places—the fate of many downtowns in the 1970s. City planners who strive to make driving and parking more convenient inevitably degrade the urban environment as a result. Besides, such efforts are detrimental to transit service. It is the planner's role not to incentivize driving, but to create a transit and pedestrian experience that makes *not driving* a pleasure.

3.12 Bicycle Network

Make all significant destinations accessible by bicycle.

San Francisco, CA: Bicycle use and safety will only increase as the city extends its bicycle network.

A proper bicycle network consists of four basic types of facilities: bicycle trails, bicycle lanes, bicycle boulevards, and shared routes. *Bicycle trails* are physically separated from higher-speed traffic. *Bicycle lanes* are demarcated by striping within medium-speed roadways. *Bicycle boulevards* are streets with low traffic volumes in which priority is given to bicyclists by traffic-calming devices and signage. Finally, *shared routes*—the majority of thoroughfares—are low-speed streets in which cars and bikes mix comfortably. While not every thoroughfare must make special provisions, bicycle networks should provide access to every important destination. The first step is to map the existing network, remembering that much of it will consist of unmarked shared routes within neighborhoods. This network should then be expanded by using the three other basic bikeway types, as contextually appropriate. The bicycle destinations should be equipped with secure parking facilities and showers available within buildings. While bicycle use is not yet widespread in the United States, this will change once adequate networks are in place.

3.13 Congestion Pricing

Establish user fees to reflect the true costs of driving.

London, UK:
A congestion pricing program has reduced traffic in the city core by 20 percent and shortened average journey time by 14 percent.

To function properly, markets require efficient feedback loops. One source of inefficiency occurs when a commodity is priced at a constant level even though its value fluctuates. Highways, tunnels, parking, and other sometimes congested, sometimes underutilized infrastructure are more valuable at times when they are in greater demand. Like public utilities, they should be priced proportionately to demand in order to flatten out spikes in use. Only with congestion-based pricing are drivers able to make choices based upon true costs, including such intangibles as tailpipe pollution and time wasted in traffic. Just as electric utilities charge more at peak hour, transportation systems should vary their pricing to discourage rush-hour use. Of course, congestion pricing is most equitable when alternatives exist, such as public transit.

3.14 Shared Vehicles

Organize car- and bicycle-sharing programs.

Washington, DC: An automobile-sharing program provides cars affordably and on demand without the expense or hassle of ownership.

In a nation obsessed with ownership, it is encouraging to see how many communitarian programs are catching on. Among the most significant are Zipcar and the other car-sharing programs that have convinced many urban dwellers to go without a personal automobile. Each Zipcar put into service results in 15 private vehicles being taken off the road. Bicycle sharing, popular in Europe, is now being introduced in several American cities. In the District of Columbia, corporate sponsorship has brought costs below $20 per year for full access to shared bicycles. Known as *product service systems*, the concept can be applied to any good that is used only periodically. While such programs are typically initiated at the grassroots level, municipalities can support them with incentives such as dedicating on-street parking spaces to communitarian car use.

The Neighborhood

The Neighborhood

Smart growth communities make the most of their context by preserving and celebrating their natural amenities. These include trees and woodlands, high points and their views, existing topography and its drainage patterns, and wetlands and their buffers. These all contribute to higher real estate value while sustaining the environment. Smart growth communities respond to climate conditions by conserving water; they preserve topsoil during the site development process; and they maintain large open spaces within easy access by linking them into natural corridors for the benefit of both wildlife and humans.

Preserving Nature

Retain and protect major natural features.

Beaufort County, SC: Existing wetlands and tree stands become great civic amenities for those neighborhoods with the foresight to preserve them.

When a site is developed, all ponds, streams, marshes, hills, tree stands, specimen trees, and other significant natural features should be preserved. As Christopher Alexander instructed, "Buildings must always be built on those parts of the land which are in the worst condition, not the best." In addition to the ecological benefits, there are many reasons to preserve the existing landscape. Natural features provide a mature sense of permanence and local character which contributes significantly to property values. Numerous studies have demonstrated that the real estate premiums resulting from preserved natural amenities far outweigh the cost of protecting them.

Celebrating Nature

Expose the natural amenities to public view.

Seaside, FL: This early new urban community owes some of its success to the many dune walkovers that announce the beach beyond.

The most valued and valuable communities do more than simply preserve their natural features; they celebrate them. Waterfronts, mountain views, forests, parks, and even golf courses are not to be hidden behind private property, but should be at least partially fronted by public spaces, thoroughfares, and walkways. It may be acceptable to sell off part of a natural vista, but never so much that it becomes invisible or inaccessible from the urbanized area. Especially important are features located at the ends of straight thoroughfares, a view shared by all of the buildings lining the street. Indeed, great plans aim roadways directly at prominent amenities such as mountain peaks or bodies of water. When a site is developed, it is tempting to privatize and sell the best views to a front row of lots for a quick windfall. Developers who resist this impulse will benefit ultimately from the increased value of all units throughout the depth of the community.

Preserving Trees

Design public places around existing trees.

Seattle, WA: Mature tree stands were retained at Othello Station, a HOPE VI
community that replaced a 1940s-era public housing project.

The preservation of trees should be a major determinant of any site plan. Among the first steps of design should be a tree survey locating specimen trees and significant tree stands which will then serve as the location of parks, greens, squares, and other public spaces. These spaces help keep site work at a distance from root mass, so that the trees do not subsequently wither and die. Linear allees and hedgerows may be assigned to avenues, again taking care to protect tree roots. Where possible, trees that cannot be maintained in their location should be transplanted in tree-save areas. This was the case at Mt. Laurel near Birmingham, Alabama, where more than 2500 trees were transplanted. A neighborhood's value is increased enormously by old growth trees, as proper canopies take a full human generation to grow.

4.4 Celebrating High Points

Assign significant hilltops to public use.

Pike Road, AL: The new village of The Waters reserves its highest ground for a chapel and meeting hall.

The high points of a site should be kept free of private development and reserved as public space or for civic buildings. Vistas to and from privileged places should not be privatized; only communal structures merit such exalted sites. Most complaints about hillside development refer not to the hillside, but to the hilltop, where private houses impinge on the natural skyline when seen from afar. As long as houses keep their roofs below the ridge, the visual damage is limited. But a well-designed civic building can enhance a hilltop with its bold silhouette.

Reducing Cut and Fill

Limit the use of the bulldozer.

Shelby County, AL: Careful scrutiny during the design process fit Mt. Laurel's roads to the difficult site.

Planners should work with the existing topography to minimize grading. Although it is easier and often cheaper to build on a flattened site, rolling terrain makes a place more memorable, while mass grading disturbs surface drainage patterns that must then be replaced by expensive underground pipes. Grading also kills large quantities of trees. In general, plans should locate the greatest density on the flattest areas and reserve steep slopes for the largest lots, which will thereby be proportionately less encumbered by buildings. A rule of thumb is to allow only single-family houses on slopes over 15 percent and to forgo development entirely on slopes over 30 percent. Plans that work with steep topography should deploy intersections that fork around center-green triangles, as these require dramatically less cut and fill than conventional right-angle intersections. Although usually associated with rural locales, such intersections have shaped beautiful urban streets in places such as Birmingham.

Maintaining the Soil

Limit erosion and soil compaction during construction.

Rosemary Beach, FL: A strict landscape code requires houses
to preserve all soil and vegetation beyond their footprint.

The healthiest soils are those maintained in their natural state. Grading plans should control erosion during and after construction, taking special care not to alter drainage or groundwater recharge areas. Engineers must design water retention/detention systems to protect streams from sedimentation. Contractors should limit soil compaction through the designation of site access routes and staging areas. Excavated topsoil should be saved and protected for reuse. Where necessary, mulch should be used to retain soil moisture during site work.

4.7 Managing Stormwater

Preserve hydrological patterns where possible.

Beaufort County, SC: In the new town of Habersham, roads are draped lightly on the landscape to limit their stormwater impacts.

The best way to manage stormwater is to follow existing drainage and percolation patterns. This is best achieved by maintaining a site's topography and allowing low areas to continue performing their role, and by using infiltration devices and permeable surfaces. As described in Tom Low's *Light Imprint Handbook*, these techniques cost less than the conventional "pipes and pits" approach, while contributing handsomely to property values. Stormwater runoff can be further reduced by placing buildings away from porous soil so that it can continue to perform its function. But these techniques are not universally appropriate. Stormwater regulations must have different standards for more urban sites. True urbanity is made impossible by regulations that enforce the generic sub-urbanism of grassy swales and on-site detention ponds, precluding the dense development that reduces sprawl.

4.8 Preserving Wetlands

Protect wetlands with upland buffers.

Middleton, WI: A 20-acre wetland park at the center of the new Middleton Hills neighborhood protects a sensitive ecosystem and provides environmental education.

Environmental standards typically disallow construction within wetlands. But more than the wetland itself must be protected if its ecosystem is to thrive. Buffers are needed to protect wetlands from erosion, nutrient loading, and the loss of the many species that require transitional habitats. Rather than just leaving wetlands untouched, plans should surround them with parks. Studies suggest that upland buffers should maintain a minimum width of 50 feet and an average width of at least 100 feet. When artificial stormwater retention ponds are created, they should be designed for maximum habitat value, with planted littoral shelves and shorelines. Islands, sandbars, and mudflats further contribute to the habitat's richness. Such new wetlands, when modeled closely on nature, can eventually function as natural ones do.

Conserving Water

Collect and reuse water, especially where it is scarce.

Austin, TX: In the dry hill country, a large cistern collects rainwater for household use.

Landscaped yards contribute mightily to water shortages in many places. Fortunately, a range of techniques now allow domestic needs to be met without wasting clean tap water. The first is xeriscape landscaping (Point 13.10) which uses less thirsty plant species. A variety of methods for harvesting water on-site can further reserve the available supply. Water collected in cisterns and ponds (flowing from terraces and rooftops) can irrigate plants. Recycling household graywater from showers and sinks, while slightly more costly, is another key strategy. Constructed wetland systems can also cleanse sewage wastewater. These cost less to build than conventional water treatment plants, conserve energy, result in lower monthly sewer charges, and provide a visual amenity and educational tool.

4.10 Urban Parks

Provide natural areas close to dwellings.

Orlando, FL: Many of the lakes in the city's historic neighborhoods are now connected by parks.

One of the worst outcomes of sprawl has been the gradual distancing of large-scale open space from urbanized areas. Most American cities that did not establish park systems by the early twentieth century now find their residents deprived of the benefits and pleasures of nature. Access to nature is a basic right, especially for those without the means to drive. Parks can be justified on an economic basis alone. Studies show that creative-class workers—those young, educated innovators who can live wherever they please, and whom every city wants to attract—consistently list ready access to nature as a dominant factor in their choice of place to live. Portland's hillside parks are among its attractions to this demographic group. Cities that wish to be competitive will establish and maintain a thorough network of parks.

4.11 Natural Corridors

Link green areas into continuous systems.

Gaithersburg, MD: The new communities of Kentlands and Lakelands (center) are shaped by the preservation of a continuous parkland system.

Large areas of nature function better for wildlife when linked. Natural corridors generally take one of two forms: wider greenways that remain outside of neighborhoods so as not to interrupt the transportation network; and narrower fingers that may extend into neighborhoods as boulevard flanks or medians. The greenways, 200 feet across or more, may be mapped at the scale of a regional plan. Where they are intersected by roads, the corridors should be equipped with "critter crossings" to enable migration and avoid roadkill. Boulevard medians, at least 20 feet wide, should provide sidewalk crossings to avoid disruption of pedestrian trajectories. Development plans should demonstrate how the green areas have been linked into a continuous system beyond the site.

The Neighborhood

Smart growth communities consist primarily of neighborhoods, each of which satisfies the ordinary daily needs of its residents within walking distance. Each neighborhood should contain a balanced mix of uses, including large and small dwellings, retail spaces, workplaces, and civic buildings. The most complete neighborhoods also provide their residents with pedestrian access to schools, day care, recreational centers, and a variety of open spaces, as well as opportunities for food production. While neighborhoods contain a wide range of dwelling types, higher densities should be encouraged because they improve the viability of nonresidential activity, including transit. Where population is too low to engender a full neighborhood, buildings should cluster to preserve the countryside. Finally, gated residential areas are not neighborhoods, and their construction should be avoided.

5.1 Mixed Use

Create neighborhoods that enable diverse activity.

Memphis, TN: Harbor Town, a first-generation new urban neighborhood, includes restaurants, shops, apartments, and a small hotel.

A neighborhood should endeavor to include a balanced mix of housing, working, shopping, recreation, and civic uses. To achieve this, specialized developers should be encouraged to joint-venture with other specialists. While a perfect balance is rarely possible, larger parcels containing single uses must be avoided. Simply put, housing subdivisions, apartment clusters, office parks, and shopping centers are the ingredients of suburban sprawl and the antithesis of smart growth. To encourage mixed use, municipalities might grant financial incentives to well-balanced neighborhoods, since they reduce traffic impact as well as infrastructure and service costs. Special consideration should also be provided to new development that re-balances adjacent areas of single use.

5.2 The 24-Hour City

Rebalance urban areas by adding missing activities.

Silver Spring, MD: A reinvigorated downtown, once suburban, now hums with nighttime activity.

The key to active street life is to create a 24-hour city, which implies an area so diverse in use that it is inhabited around the clock. Living, working, shopping, schooling, and socializing must coexist in close proximity. No one such activity can really flourish in the absence of another, as they are all mutually reinforcing. Such diversity contributes to safety by ensuring that areas don't empty out at night. As recommended by Jane Jacobs almost 50 years ago, revitalization should begin by reinstating this urban balance. In most downtowns, housing is underrepresented, so cities should make special efforts to bring more apartments and rowhouses into their urban cores.

Housing Diversity

Include a full range of housing in each neighborhood.

Atlanta, GA: Apartments, rowhouses, and single-family homes are seamlessly integrated at Glenwood Park.

For many reasons, a healthy neighborhood includes a wide range of dwelling types. First, authentic community social networks depend on the presence of a diversity of ages and incomes. Second, affordable housing provides a healthier social environment when it is distributed rather than concentrated. Third, it is more efficient to live in the same neighborhood as one's doctor or schoolteacher, not to mention one's adult child or elderly parent. Fourth, life-cycle housing allows residents to move up economically without moving out; one can upsize or downsize without leaving established social networks. "Lifelong communities" (Point 14.5) generate the strongest support systems. Finally, a diversity of housing options allows developers to access multiple market segments, thereby achieving faster product absorption. Therefore, neighborhoods should include many, if not all, of the following: rental apartments, condominiums, live/work buildings, rowhouses, cottages, houses, and mansions. Even small developments suffer when they limit housing to just one or two types.

Retail Distribution

Satisfy daily shopping needs within each neighborhood.

New Town St. Charles, MO: At the very least, each neighborhood should place a corner market within walking distance of most dwellings.

All neighborhoods should include retail space; the amount depends upon the neighborhood's size, density, and location relative to transportation. Neighborhoods of 300 or more dwellings and/or jobs should provide a viable corner store at minimum. Where justified by its location on the regional traffic network, a neighborhood can center on a set of "main street" stores. These shops do best when they flank both sides of a low-speed thoroughfare. Businesses such as corner stores and cafés—*third places*, to use Ray Oldenburg's term—form the social center of a community. They should be considered as infrastructure and initially subsidized by the developer if necessary. Developers who have provided a well-run corner store will vouch that it is a cherished amenity and a great marketing device. It is less likely to require financial assistance if combined with a café and the neighborhood post office, where residents go daily to pick up mail. In any case, such an amenity requires no more subsidy than the pool, clubhouse, staffed security gate, or landscape maintenance crew typical of most suburban developments. Management is also important, as shoppers tend to favor locally owned businesses anchored by known national brands, a mix that will not occur when left to chance.

Workplace Distribution

Provide the potential for jobs within each neighborhood.

Atlanta, GA: Offices and apartments above shops create Riverside's mixed-use town center—a development originally planned as disconnected single-use pods.

The ideal neighborhood has as many jobs as it does workers; the resulting "jobs-housing balance" is the single greatest remedy for peak-hour traffic congestion. Of course, if the neighborhood has good transit connections to major employment centers, it could contain very few jobs while still contributing to a regional balance. While most neighborhood jobs will be in offices, light manufacturing and artisan uses can be included as long as they do not create a nuisance. The majority of workspace should be located at or near the neighborhood center, where there is easy access to support services, meals, and transit. In addition to offices located above stores, live/work buildings and home occupations should be encouraged as a way of balancing residential areas and incubating new businesses that may not yet be able to afford proper commercial rents.

5.6 Civic Sites

Designate civic sites in each neighborhood.

Davidson, NC: The extension to this historic town
includes sites reserved for public buildings.

Civic buildings will emerge naturally as a community matures, but only if provisions are made for them early in the planning process. Each neighborhood should reserve at least one public tract for the essential meeting hall. Typically, this site is located at the neighborhood center—perhaps associated with a public green or square—where the civic building can share parking and transit access with complementary workday uses. The best locations occupy high ground or terminate the axial vistas so that even small buildings are enhanced to the preeminence that befits a civic function. While waiting for a civic building to become viable, its site can be landscaped as a public open space.

Neighborhood Schools

Size and locate schools to be within walking distance.

Gaithersburg, MD: Rachel Carson Elementary
allows Kentlands' kids to walk to school.

Until the 1970s, the majority of American children walked to school. Today, less than 15 percent do, mostly because they can't. To help correct this problem, new schools must be sized and located to be reached easily on foot or bicycle. Elementary schools must be within 1 mile of most dwellings, and high schools not much farther. When placed in neighborhoods, these facilities can double as after-hours community and recreational centers. Unfortunately, school boards continue to replace small local schools—often historic—with megafacilities to which no child can walk. Large schools may be more efficient in terms of construction and management, but increased busing quickly absorbs the savings, further dwarfed by the hidden subsidy of parental driving. In the state of Maine, school busing costs have increased sixfold over the past 25 years, despite a decrease in the number of students. Most school consolidation arguments ignore three facts: smaller schools produce higher-performing students; walking to school produces healthier children; and busing and parental chauffeuring exacerbate rush-hour traffic. School authorities should eliminate any standards that discourage small schools and any legal barriers that make them unavailable for after-hours community use.

5.8 Support Services

Provide day care and recreation in each neighborhood.

San Francisco, CA: Britton Courts housing includes
social services such as day care on site.

A significant portion of the traffic congestion in suburban communities results from parents driving children to distant child care centers and play areas. Since such facilities can be small, each neighborhood can contain at least one, typically located at or near the neighborhood center. Placing day care in close proximity to shopping and work enables time-saving multipurpose trips. These sites should be reserved early in the planning process. Similarly, swimming pools and indoor recreation centers must be carefully allocated in neighborhood plans if they are to be within pedestrian range of most dwellings. These should be planned in conjunction with local schools, which can share them.

Local Open Space

Provide a variety of public places in each neighborhood.

Douglasville, GA: The new Tributary neighborhood contains a full range of open-space types, all accessible on foot.

As Charles Moore used to say, "When the revolution starts, there should be no question of where to go." For this reason, every neighborhood should include a plaza, green, or square as its social center. In addition, each neighborhood should provide its residents with convenient access to a range of more explicitly programmed open spaces. Pocket parks or small playgrounds should be located so that children need not cross any major streets to reach them. Active recreational parks with ball fields should be located within access of bicycling children, not clustered in megafacilities as is current practice. These parks can be associated with schools and/or green corridors between neighborhoods. Community gardens and nature trails may also be located in these parks. In a well-designed regional plan, every dwelling is located within an easy bicycle ride of a continuous park system, so that a day of hiking or trailbiking need not begin with a drive.

5.10 Housing Density

Develop as much housing as the market will bear.

Washington, DC: The Jefferson at Thomas Circle provides 150 units per acre in a contextually appropriate manner.

The "D word" is a contentious issue among planners and citizens. High density is too often seen as a panacea to the ills of sprawl, when in fact it is only one of many factors contributing to smart growth. For example, Tyson's Corner, Virginia—a sprawl icon—is quite dense, but fails as a pedestrian environment because it lacks a walkable neighborhood structure. All else being equal, however, higher-density developments do mitigate sprawl in several ways. Because they place more people on less land, they help to preserve open space. And since density supports transit, they reduce dependence on the automobile. For these reasons, Manhattan can be considered the most sustainable place in America. Still, as many people seem to prefer the "American dream" of a house on its own yard, municipalities must allow such houses to be built as part of diverse neighborhoods. Only if urbanism is practical, walkable, and convivial will density be tolerated by buyers, neighbors, and elected officials. Urbanism must deliver on its promise of convenience and street life as compensation for the absence of a suburban yard.

Nearby Farms

Grow and sell food at the neighborhood level.

Grass Valley, CA: The Loma Rica organic farm
provides food security to a new community.

After the era of cheap oil, America's metropolitan regions will need to
be more self-sufficient, not least in terms of food production. Transport
costs will revalue commodities close at hand. Whenever a neighborhood
is planned, significant open space should be set aside for growing food,
whether or not there is a present demand for it. In terms of enhancing real
estate value, community-supported agriculture promises to be the golf
course of the twenty-first century. People are increasingly willing to pay
more for local, fresh, healthy food. At the other end of the economic scale,
many low-income communities are already suffering from being "food
deserts," shunned by supermarkets and served only by expensive mini-
marts and unhealthy fast-food chains. This circumstance contributes to
our national epidemics of obesity and diabetes. Beyond supporting food
growing, policy is needed at the regional level so that markets selling
decent food are rewarded for locating in urban areas.

5.12 Clustering Houses

In rural areas, build houses in compact groupings.

Ashton, MD: In a creative interpretation of existing 2-acre-lot zoning, the hamlet of Wyndcrest clusters 26 houses to preserve surrounding open space.

Clustering refers to the practice of preserving open space by locating housing at higher density on a portion of its site. This concept underlies the practice of Conservation Subdivision Design, an established technique for maximizing open space while limiting infrastructure costs. It is an ideal approach for sites which have large-lot development rights and not enough housing allocation to become full mixed-use neighborhoods. Many jurisdictions would welcome clustering, but few have zoning in place that actually allows, let alone encourages, it. To support this practice, municipalities must provide density bonuses that allow clustered projects to yield a return on investment equal to or greater than that of the legal large-lot alternative. The degree of incentive will vary from place to place, but only under such a policy will clustering become a common practice.

Open Communities

Do not allow limited-access developments.

Anywhere, USA: According to the sign, not even pedestrians are allowed to enter this gated enclave.

More than 4 million American households are located within gated communities. Although somewhat on the wane, these enclaves are still being built. While it is possible to object to such developments on cultural or ethical principles, there are a number of strictly technical reasons why they are not considered smart growth. First, they disrupt the road network, acting as huge cul-de-sacs and impeding an efficient, distributive transportation network. Second, they don't mix uses and thus contribute inordinate amounts of traffic to surrounding road systems. Finally, they generally provide only a narrow range of housing types and therefore forestall the socioeconomic robustness that accrues to places with a full spectrum of ages and incomes. By this logic, there is less wrong with a gated community if it is complete and self-sufficient, such as the walled towns of the middle ages, but these rarely occur these days. Instead, the gates are provided less for internal safety than as a marketing ploy that serves only to reinforce socioeconomic segregation.

The Neighborhood

Neighborhoods are by definition scaled to the pedestrian. A typical neighborhood has a dense center containing a main public space. Smaller parks and playgrounds are scattered throughout. Neighborhoods are "zoned" not by use but by compatible building types, which are often enforced through a form-based code. Each neighborhood should be planned to support efficient transit use—regardless of whether it exists yet—and designed to allow small-scale food sourcing throughout. To help better meet these criteria, the U.S. Green Building Council rating system has been expanded to include neighborhood design.

6.1 Neighborhood Size

Design neighborhoods around a five-minute walk.

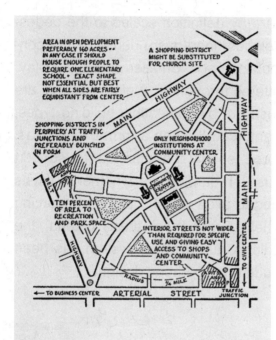

Clarence Perry's neighborhood unit diagram of 1929 clarified standards that have existed as long as humans have built cities.

The neighborhood is the fundamental increment for designing and understanding villages, towns, and cities. Its size corresponds to the five-minute walk, or "pedestrian shed," averaging one-quarter mile from edge to center. Most pre-automobile communities are organized on this basis, and most new communities, to be walkable, should be as well. Large sites to be developed should first be divided conceptually into pedestrian sheds. This structure places the majority of households within a short walk of a mixed-use center. Of course, most neighborhoods will not be round or square, as geographical circumstances often distort the outline. In some cases, neighborhood centers will migrate to a neighborhood edge, due to the need to locate retail on the most traveled thoroughfares. Once determined, the neighborhood structure provides the framework for organizing all aspects of the plan. It is also a useful tool for revitalizing older cities, as the search for the neighborhood structure will often reveal a historic community's submerged organizational framework.

Neighborhood Organization

Determine a center and an edge for each neighborhood.

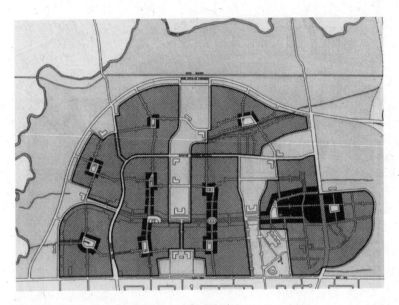

Markham, Ontario: Cornell, a 2400-acre urban extension, shows the discipline of the neighborhood structure.

Each neighborhood is defined principally by its center and secondarily by its edge. This combination of focus and limit helps to establish the functional and social identity of the community. While a well-defined edge could be considered a luxury, a clear center is a necessity. The neighborhood center should be marked by a public space such as a plaza, square, or green; the appropriate type depends upon the local culture. Paved plazas are the most urban, while naturalistic greens are more rural. The edge of the neighborhood can vary radically in character. In towns and cities—defined as agglomerations of neighborhoods—the edge is often marked by boulevards or parkways that allow through-traffic to circumvent the neighborhood, or by main streets that take advantage of this traffic to support retail activity. In villages—defined as a single neighborhood standing free in nature—the edge is typically formed by houses and farms that interface with the rural surroundings.

6.3 Pocket Parks

Locate playgrounds within a short walk of most homes.

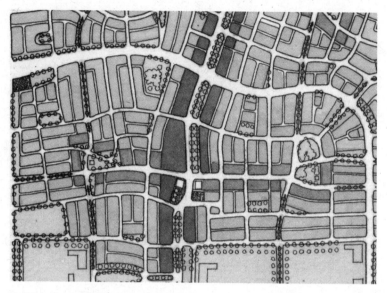

Markham, Ontario: Each neighborhood of Cornell
has playgrounds within easy reach of children.

Within the neighborhood, playgrounds and tot lots should be distributed so as to be within a two-minute walk of most households. When they are spaced at this distance, a typical neighborhood will contain a small handful. Each is usually about a quarter-acre in size, containing hard and soft surfaces, benches, and play equipment under ample tree cover. While a pocket park may occupy an undeveloped home lot, it is best placed at a significant location such as a staggered intersection or vista termination. It is convenient to place day care facilities adjacent to these playgrounds. Although they can be provided and maintained by a municipal parks department, pocket parks can also be funded through neighborhood associations.

Open-Space Types

Provide a range of familiar types of public space.

Celebration, FL: Savannah Square meets the
requirements of a first-rate urban space.

If they are to succeed in their function, most open spaces should correspond to historically evolved types. Parks, greens, squares, and plazas
all follow specific patterns that have been proven to work. For example,
a *square* is typically 1 to 5 acres and surrounded on at least three sides
by streets lined with buildings. It holds formal tree rows at its perimeter
and may have a sunny, open center. It contains paved walks for strolling
and grassy areas for play. Its walks follow the desired pedestrian trajectories across the site, so that people will use it as a shortcut. If any
of these elements are missing, it will function less well as a square.
Similar definitions could be written for the full range of open-space
types. Their design should be based on well-tested models, as the
sad experience of so many unused public spaces shows the risks that
accompany invention.

Form-Based Zoning

Locate buildings by their type rather than their use.

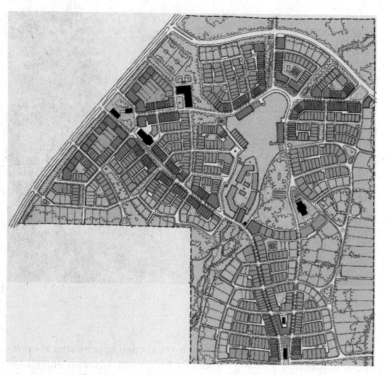

Montgomery, AL: The regulating plan for Hampstead allocates building types according to the logic of the rural-to-urban transect.

Smart growth codes based on building configuration should replace conventional zoning based on land use. In these codes (Point 12.1), big buildings are located among other big buildings, midsized buildings among other midsized buildings, and so on. Generally, from the neighborhood center to the neighborhood edge, buildings become less tall and occupy less of their lots. These different building forms imply and induce different land uses without making them the law. The coexistence within a neighborhood of multiple building types avoids physical and social monocultures and allows for natural evolution in use, decreasing the likelihood of demolition. Compatible setbacks and parking location also lead to harmony despite a potential variety of mixed and changing uses. With rare exception, streets should be symmetrical, with the same building types on both sides and the zoning transitions at midblock, along the rear of the lots, where they are invisible. Consistent streetscapes thus result from inconsistent blocks.

6.6 Transit Orientation

Plan neighborhoods and corridors to support transit.

Minneapolis, MN: The new Hiawatha line has outpaced ridership estimates, in part because of the excellent pedestrian environment flanking its route.

Whether service is available or planned, neighborhood centers should be designed to be transit-ready. Because every transit trip begins and ends with walking, the pedestrian-oriented neighborhood structure intrinsically supports transit. Riding a bus or a tram becomes much more popular when reached via a pleasant walk. The location of transit stops at the centers of pedestrian sheds implies a transit loop that links them, and also connects to a downtown or a larger transportation hub. Studies show that residents will readily walk 5 minutes to a bus stop and 10 minutes to a rail stop. This suggests that while buses can link neighborhood centers, light rail could be located more efficiently at the seams between neighborhoods, with each stop potentially serving four neighborhoods within a 10-minute pedestrian shed. These seams then become transit corridors for the highest densities of housing, retail, and offices.

6.7 Edible Gardens

Encourage food production everywhere by everyone.

Seattle, WA: The new High Point neighborhood
is socially anchored by its community gardens.

Neighborhoods should offer opportunities for growing food across the entire rural-to-urban transect, roughly organized as follows:

- Small farms of 1 to 5 acres, located at the rural edge, employ workers to provide food for the region.
- Yard gardens on suburban house lots help families in less urban zones to satisfy their own food needs.
- Container gardens, such as window boxes and balcony and roof gardens, reduce dependence on shipped produce in more urban areas.
- Community gardens can do the same for residents of mid- and high-rise buildings in the urban core.

The neighborhood design and the building layouts should work in tandem to ensure that food-growing opportunities are available for the sustenance and pleasure of all residents.

6.8 The LEED-ND Rating System

Measure sustainability with this useful tool.

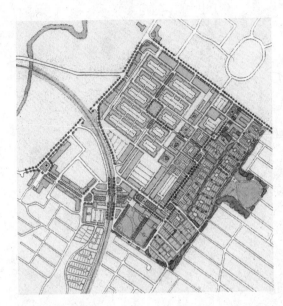

Woodridge, NJ: Retrofitting an aircraft factory into a transit-oriented neighborhood will likely earn Wesmont Station LEED-ND Silver status.

Claims of sustainability should be verified. The principal standard currently available for doing so is the Leadership in Energy and Environmental Design rating system for Neighborhood Development (LEED-ND). A joint effort of the Congress for the New Urbanism, the Natural Resources Defense Council, and the U.S. Green Building Council, LEED-ND is the community-scale expansion of the established LEED rating system which has previously been limited to the scale of the building. Using this tool, municipalities, developers, and prospective residents will be able to objectively determine the degree to which proposed projects embody smart growth principles. For buildings, LEED has demonstrated the value of a clear and enforceable metric in construction practice. Just as some governments are now requiring LEED certification for new buildings, it is expected that LEED-ND will become a municipal standard for controlling the urban design of large-scale development. Given its enormous potential impact, the results must be continuously monitored and the metric updated to minimize unintended consequences.

The Street

The Street

Smart growth is structured on a network of thorough-fares that connect wherever feasible. This network consists of relatively small blocks continually lined by buildings, so that no neighborhood street is relegated strictly to the movement of vehicles. Because high-speed collector roads are rare, skywalks and underground passages are unnecessary. Vistas down streets are generally kept short and deflected in memorable ways to slow traffic. Streets that curve tend to maintain their general cardinal direction for the sake of orientation. For gas stations and other necessary but noxious uses, an A-B street network allocates such activities away from a primary network of superior pedestrian quality.

The Network

Organize streets in a clear network.

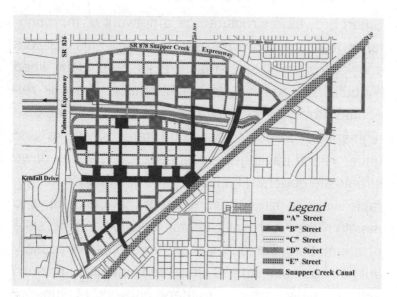

Legend

▬▬ "A" Street
▬▬ "B" Street
········ "C" Street
▨▨ "D" Street
▥▥ "E" Street
▬▬ Snapper Creek Canal

Kendall, FL: Streets replace parking lots in what has become
a new downtown for Miami's southern suburbs.

Thoroughfares should be organized into an interconnected and hierar-
chical network. The largest thoroughfares should connect to the urban
center, dividing developed areas into neighborhoods. Within each neighborhood, shorter and narrower streets should be detailed for local traffic
at slower speeds. The neighborhood's network, while emphasizing its
center, provides multiple routes to and from all destinations, so that
traffic is dispersed and backups are limited. Multiple routes also benefit
pedestrians: people who live in neighborhoods with finely grained street
networks have been shown to walk more, use transit more, and drive
less than those who live in conventional large-block and cul-de-sac
suburbs. This arrangement is particularly useful for those too young,
too old, or too poor to depend on the car for their mobility.

Connected Thoroughfares

Do not allow dead-end streets.

Anywhere, USA: While potentially appealing when considered alone, each cul-de-sac undermines the function of the overall system.

Neighborhoods should rarely contain cul-de-sacs. Because dead-end systems reduce the number of through-streets, those streets that do connect become overburdened. By the same logic, urban street closures are usually a bad idea. In a truly porous network, each street receives enough traffic to keep it active and supervised, but not so much as to make it unpleasant for pedestrians. Cul-de-sacs are also a problem for emergency vehicles, since they provide only one path to each destination, which might be blocked by traffic or an accident. Because they lengthen trips, cul-de-sacs add to the costs of policing, busing, and mail delivery. Finally, studies have shown that fewer social ties develop when pedestrian connectivity is limited. For these reasons, Charlotte has made cul-de-sacs illegal, and the Virginia Department of Transportation now requires connectivity in its residential subdivision standards.

Connections Beyond

Connect neighborhoods to adjacent roads and sites.

Gaithersburg, MD: When designed, Kentlands (left) kept connections open for future development. Lakelands (right) took the cue.

The need for connectivity is not limited within the neighborhood. Any development will have a negative traffic impact if it is disconnected from the developments around it. To avoid functioning as a giant cul-de-sac, a neighborhood should have regularly spaced streets in and out wherever they are not impeded by natural obstructions, inviolable private property, or the intersection-spacing requirements of state transportation departments. (This final factor usually merits challenge, as widely spaced intersections create more traffic congestion than they mitigate.) Any street that arrives on a developable property should be continued through the development. And any site surrounded by potentially developable land should be planned with regularly spaced street easements in place, allowing connections into future development.

7.4 Block Size

Keep blocks small, especially downtown.

Alys Beach, FL:
From north to south,
according to the logic
of the transect, midsize
rural blocks give way to
smaller urban blocks:

A permeating street network is the result of small blocks. Jane Jacobs observed that the most walkable parts of towns and cities are found where blocks are the smallest. Downtown Portland's blocks are only 200 feet square, and Savannah's original wards have 530 intersections per square mile. Blocks in new neighborhoods should typically range from 1000 to 2000 feet in perimeter. Generally, blocks become smaller from the rural edge to the urban center. A justified exception to this rule is an urban center block containing a hidden parking lot within. Such blocks should be planned to be subdivided if parking eventually is structured or reduced. In lower-density areas, blocks may be made somewhat longer if they are cut through by pedestrian passages. Pedestrian passages are also useful for continuing street trajectories where slopes make street connections impossible.

Sidewalk Substitutes

Avoid building skywalks or tunnels.

Miami, FL: Even on the nicest of days, skywalks linking parking garages to office buildings absorb sidewalk activity.

A futuristic idea not yet fully discredited, skywalks and tunnels are sometimes still considered in urban locations. They are often promoted by downtown developers who wish to provide a protected path from parking garages to office buildings or other destinations. Such measures are only appropriate when no other safe passage is possible, as they rob sidewalks of pedestrian life and hurt retail businesses. This segregation by levels is often just a matter of segregation by class, with only the poor and their struggling shops left at street level. Indeed, removing some of the pedestrians from a potentially unsafe street only makes it more dangerous. While sidewalk substitutes may sometimes be justified by fast-moving traffic, the more economical solution is to design and signalize streets for lower speeds. Poor climate alone is rarely justification for sidewalk substitutes, as some of the world's best walking cities, such as New Orleans and Quebec City, still attract pedestrians during many months of truly miserable weather.

Designed Vistas

Keep most vistas short, and terminate them memorably.

Huntsville, AL: Vistas of specific character add a sense
of place to the public realm at Providence.

While many successful places have straight streets, new neighborhoods
can improve pedestrian safety, comfort, and enjoyment with a street
network that provides deflected vistas. Vistas that run straight and far
into the distance cause drivers to speed. They also result in street spaces
that do not feel adequately enclosed. In contrast, street networks that
include staggered intersections, deflections, and slight curves improve
spatial definition and orientation by creating memorable visual events.
Terminated vistas provide honorific sites appropriate to civic places. In
the best-designed neighborhoods, few street vistas are more than 1000
feet long, and most are carefully aimed at a natural feature, a public
space, or a well-placed building. When a street vista terminates on a
building, it should reciprocate by placing a special architectural element
on axis. Regulating plans for new neighborhoods should indicate all
significant vista terminations in order to prompt building designers to
respond appropriately.

7.7 Curvilinear Streets

Bend streets with restraint.

Anywhere, USA: In suburban areas, arbitrarily
curved streets are ubiquitous and disorienting.

As noted, one way to deflect a vista gracefully is to allow the street to
bend. Unfortunately, this technique has become so exaggerated and
overused that most new subdivisions consist of nothing but mindlessly
curving streets. These are disorienting to both residents and visitors,
first because the arcs are all so similar, and second because they fail to
maintain any cardinal direction. If one enters a street heading north, for
example, it is confusing to find oneself randomly heading east, south,
and west. To avoid this outcome, curves should be used with discretion,
and curving streets should maintain the same general orientation over
their entire trajectory. The only exception is on steep topography, where
switchback roads are needed to climb slopes.

Urban Triage

Establish distinct networks of walkable streets.

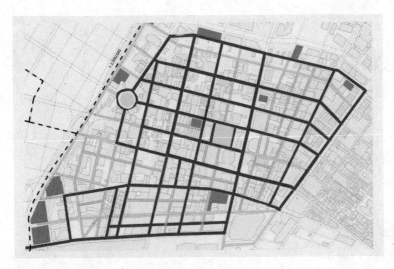

New Orleans, LA: An A-B grid designates a network of frontages (blue) held
to a pedestrian-friendly standard, while another (tan) remains car-oriented.

Even the best neighborhoods must accommodate elements that are
intrinsically hostile to pedestrian life. Among these are drive-throughs,
gas stations, blank walls, and car lots, all of which should be located in
districts beyond the neighborhood edge. But when they cannot be so
relegated—usually when rehabilitating an urban area—they should be
carefully allocated through the use of an A-B street network. An alter-
nating A-B grid does not banish pedestrian-hostile uses, but places them
on secondary streets. This system is a sort of urban triage, relaxing
pedestrian quality in some places so that other places may become
truly excellent. Streets in downtown areas should be realistically rated
A or B based upon their present viability as pedestrian routes. The A
streets can then be held to a higher standard of urban performance,
typically through the use of a form-based code, and given first priority
for streetscape improvements. Where the two systems must cross—
like a tartan plaid—the A streets should trump the others to form a
continuous system, so that one need not walk along B street frontages.
This urban triage approach may appear unfair to B street properties, but
they too will retain commercial value, as there is unfortunately always a
market for automobile-oriented uses.

The Street

Smart growth neighborhoods contain a range of thoroughfare types, most of which are designed to be equitable for the pedestrian, the bicycle, and the automobile. This is accomplished by calming traffic through a combination of appropriate design speeds, complex intersections, tight corner curb radii, and on-street parking. One-way and multilane thoroughfares are absent in all but the most urban areas, as these can undermine walkability. A rich variety of available thoroughfare types is organized according to their urban context, including avenues, boulevards, streets, roads, alleys, lanes, passages, and paths. Free-flow, slow-flow, and yield-flow design geometries further modulate driver speed and pedestrian comfort.

Complete Streets

Design for pedestrians and bicyclists as well as automobiles.

New York, NY: A commitment to pedestrian and bicycle accommodation led to a 35% increase in bicycle use from 2007 to 2008.

For some 60 years now, most American streets have been designed with the sole objective of moving cars. As a result, pedestrian and bicycle use has declined, as has the viability of closely enfronting urban buildings. In addition to being traffic conduits, streets are public spaces and perhaps the primary location of American civic life. Thoroughfares other than highways—especially streets within neighborhoods—should be designed as places of gathering. This requires the interdisciplinary participation of engineers, planners, architects, landscape architects, and utility companies. The resulting thoroughfares will typically provide narrow (slower-speed) travel lanes, bicycle facilities, on-street parking, continuous tree cover, ample sidewalks, appropriate street furniture and lighting, as well as supportive building frontages. When streets become pleasant places, more people are likely to leave the car at home.

Design Speed

Engineer neighborhood streets to low speeds.

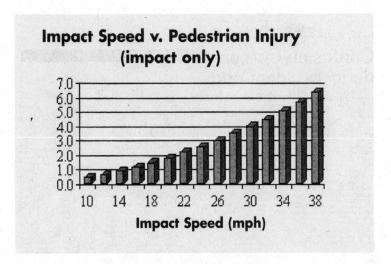

Impact Speed v. Pedestrian Injury (impact only)

With a severity of 6 equaling fatality, even slight increases over 20 miles per hour can contribute dramatically to injuries.

The speed of vehicles is critical to pedestrian safety and comfort. At 20 miles per hour, a pedestrian has a 95 percent chance of surviving a collision, compared to only 10 percent at 40 mph. The important element of eye contact between motorists and pedestrians only occurs at lower speeds, as does the safe intermingling of bicycles. Unfortunately, simply posting a speed limit is not an adequate approach, as many drivers will drive at the perceived safe speed on roadways designed for higher velocity. The most effective way to control vehicular speed is by narrowing lane widths, avoiding long straightaways, introducing on-street parking, and providing points of visual friction. These factors contribute to what engineers call *design speed*. It is now standard practice to design thoroughfares for velocities well above the posted limit, supposedly to protect speeding drivers. Far from improving safety, this approach endangers pedestrians, cyclists, and drivers alike. While higher speeds are appropriate on highways, street design within neighborhoods should physically induce speeds of 25 mph or less. As of this writing, a half-dozen British cities have mandated 20 mph speed limits in their downtowns.

Complex Geometries

Allow challenging intersections to calm traffic.

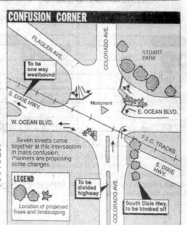

The Miami Herald

Confusion Corner defies accident odds

By NAFTALI BENDAVID
Herald Staff Writer

STUART — There are some things no one can fully explain: Stonehenge. The Bermuda Triangle. The inter-relationship of the universe's four basic forces.

And Confusion Corner.

Stuart residents are proud of the mystique of Confusion Corner, that tangled mess in downtown Stuart where seven streets — plus a railroad track — meet without the aid of a traffic light.

The mystery is how the Corner can channel so much traffic through a labyrinthine maze of asphalt, sending every driver where he wants to go without any traffic signals, and still have one of the lowest accident rates of any intersection in the region.

"It shouldn't work but it does, and I would hate to lose whatever it is that makes it work," said Stuart City Commissioner Joan Jefferson.

Despite the almost supernatural powers attributed to Confusion Cor-

undergo its first significant alteration in years.

The city is spending $238,000 to build landscaped islands where East Ocean and West Ocean Boulevards pour into the Corner, as well as a median strip on Colorado Avenue.

And South Dixie Highway will be closed off to prevent motorists on that street from shooting across Confusion Corner, a highly dangerous maneuver.

Responding to public sentiment, the City Commission rejected a more substantial change that would have allowed a direct left turn from East Ocean Boulevard onto Colorado Avenue, eliminating the bizarre S-turn maneuver that is a rite of initiation for new Stuart residents.

"If it works, then we really shouldn't be messing with it. How can you improve it?" said City Commissioner Denny Arnold. "If you can't prove to me you can improve

Counter to conventional wisdom, the most complicated roadways are often the safest.

Forks, staggered intersections, triangles, roundabouts, and other irregular geometries could once be found in towns and cities everywhere. With technocratic standardization, intersections have been reduced to a limited selection of simple configurations, essentially right angles. Evidence suggests that, contrary to expectations, these intersections create a false sense of safety and contribute to the number and severity of accidents. Further studies indicate that some of our nation's most complicated intersections—especially those without signalization—experience the lowest accident rates. While it would be counterproductive to discard all simple configurations, the existing repertoire of approved geometries must be expanded. When combined with narrow streets, short blocks, and tight curb radii (Point 8.4), complex thoroughfares create a self-policing environment that is safer for both drivers and pedestrians. It is the prohibition of these essential traffic-calming techniques that has led to the advent of more aggressive measures such as speed bumps, bulb-outs, and chicanes, needed to hobble drivers on unchallenging streets.

8.4 Curb Radii

Limit the sweep of the curbs at intersections.

Then versus now: tight corners used to make pedestrian crossing easy.
The new standards increase crossing distances and speed up cars.

Conventional public works standards specify ample curb radii at intersections so that long vehicles such as trailer trucks may turn the corners easily. These sweeping curbs do ease turning, but at the cost of forcing pedestrians to walk longer distances in front of cars that need not slow down as they turn. The result is an unnecessarily dangerous and uncomfortable environment. For this reason, the curb radii of new or rebuilt streets should be no larger than necessary to accommodate the turning motions of the largest vehicle that will use them regularly, most often a garbage truck. Within neighborhoods, where low-speed travel is encouraged, such vehicles can be expected to temporarily encroach into the opposing travel lane when making a right turn—particularly emergency trucks, which have sirens to warn the oncoming traffic. The largest vehicles, such as moving vans, should be expected to make three-point turns, since streets oversized to satisfy these rare visitors fail to satisfy regular users. As long as reasonable access is provided, curb radii of 15, 10, and even 5 feet can be appropriate. Generally, the more urban the area, the smaller the curb radius; for curbless rural roads with scarce pedestrians, corner radii as large as 25 feet are acceptable.

8.5 On-Street Parking

Allow on-street parking in all but rural areas.

West Palm Beach, FL: Parallel parking serves the businesses of City Place while shielding shoppers from moving traffic.

On-street parking provides many benefits. It slows down drivers, who are instinctively watchful of other cars in the roadway; it protects pedestrians from traffic with a thick steel barrier of cars along the sidewalk; it reduces the demand for on-site parking, decreasing the amount of parking lot pavement; and it increases sidewalk activity as drivers walk from car to destination. For these reasons, on-street parking should again become a standard part of the engineer's repertoire. Depending on use and density, parking should be provided on both sides of commercial streets, and on one or both sides of residential streets. Parallel parking is preferable, but the greater capacity of head-in (or rear-in) parking may be justified on retail streets. For retrofitting existing conditions, adding on-street parking can narrow roadways that were built too wide. On-street parking must count toward satisfying parking requirements, or developers will not provide it. Parking lanes are usually marked with a stripe on through-streets, but unmarked on local streets.

One-Way and Multilane Streets

Avoid wide and simplistic street systems.

Davenport, IA: To help revitalize its downtown, the city's transportation plan is reverting its speedy one-way streets back to two-way.

One-way streets ease traffic flow at the expense of pedestrian safety and comfort. The absence of opposing traffic makes drivers less cautious and speeding easier. One-way streets along commuting routes can also damage retail activity by providing merchants with either morning or evening trade, but not both. Finally, they limit the effectiveness of the street network, increase travel distances with around-the-block maneuvers, and can make navigation frustrating. They are justified only to ease flow in areas of extremely high density, 75 units per acre or more. Similarly, streets with more than one lane in each direction make sense only in such density. A typical travel lane can handle 700 cars per hour, so streets experiencing considerably less than 1400 cars at peak hour should not be widened beyond two lanes. Cities with multilane one-way systems should consider reverting to two-way travel, as it tends to help revitalize struggling areas.

Context-Responsive Thoroughfares

Correlate street types to the neighborhood structure.

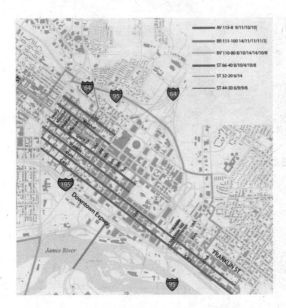

AV 115-8 9/11/10/10|	
BR 111-100 14/11/11/11/3|	
BV 110-80 8/10/14/14/10/8	
ST 66-40 8/10/4/10/8	
ST 32-20 6/14	
ST 44-30 6/9/9/6	

Richmond, VA: A new plan for downtown assigns six different thoroughfare types, each in support of its urban context.

Most subdivision ordinances offer very few thoroughfare types, typically related to function: arterials, collectors, subcollectors, and locals. Smart growth neighborhoods contain a wider variety of designs organized according to both function and context. These include the following:

- *Avenues and boulevards*: longer-range thoroughfares that typically connect neighborhood centers or skirt their edges.
- *Free-flow streets and roads*: thoroughfares with enough through-traffic to require a full-width travel lane in each direction.
- *Slow-flow streets and roads*: thoroughfares with narrower travel lanes to carry local traffic.
- *Yield-flow streets and roads*: thoroughfares with little enough traffic to allow a single lane to handle movement in both directions.
- *Alleys and lanes*: service thoroughfares that provide access to the backs of commercial and residential lots.
- *Passages and paths*: thoroughfares for pedestrian and bicycle access.

These thoroughfares are described more fully in the pages ahead.

Avenues and Boulevards

Assign regional thoroughfares to their proper context.

Gaithersburg, MD: Tschiffeley Square Road is an avenue
that connects two neighborhood centers at Kentlands.

Avenues and boulevards are higher-capacity thoroughfares that often connect neighborhood centers or skirt neighborhood edges. Both types contain planted medians, typically 10 to 20 feet wide, that sometimes allow stacking of turning vehicles at intersections. Avenues usually connect neighborhood centers and often terminate on civic buildings or spaces. Boulevards, in contrast, usually run along neighborhood edges and lack vista terminations, since they carry mostly through-traffic. The most urban boulevard design, found in cities such as Washington and Paris, has a pair of tree-planted medians flanking a central roadway, creating slower slip streets that buffer and give access to building frontages. High-volume boulevards can effectively replace highways, as has happened with San Francisco's Central Freeway. Dimensionally, avenues correspond to the standards of free-flow traffic, with 10-foot-wide travel lanes and 8-foot-wide parking lanes, while boulevards may be several feet wider to allow slightly faster flow.

Free-Flow Streets and Roads

Design high-volume thoroughfares for free flow.

Hillsboro, OR: This mixed-use street at Orenco Station
is designed for free movement but not for speeding.

Free-flow thoroughfares are streets and roads that carry enough traffic
to warrant a full-size travel lane in each direction. The number of thoroughfares of this type depends on the density. In some neighborhoods,
none may be required, while in urban downtowns, all thoroughfares
should be designed for free flow. Free-flow dimensions are 10-foot-wide
travel lanes and 8-foot-wide parking lanes. Typical free-flow streets,
then, measure either 36 feet wide (parking both sides) or 28 feet wide
(parking one side). These measurements and all others listed here are
taken from curb face to curb face, as drivers tend to park in gutter pans.
Roads are rural; they are distinguished from streets by the absence of
a curb. Free-flow roads are 20 feet wide, since parking occurs off the
pavement.

Slow-Flow Streets and Roads

Design local thoroughfares for slow flow.

Woodbridge, VA: A slow-flow street at Belmont Bay provides access to rowhouses.

Slow-flow streets and roads handle limited through-traffic while providing access to housing of moderate density. As useful as these are for cars, they are also the principal public spaces of their communities, but they can function as such only with lower vehicular speeds. The travel lanes must therefore be narrower than on free-flow streets—8 or 9 feet wide—and can be unstriped. When two cars approach each other, they must go slow or risk contact. The parking lanes can be 7 feet wide, marked or unmarked, and the overall street width is usually quite modest: as little as 24 feet with parking on one side, or 30 feet with parking on both sides. A slow-flow road, with parking off-pavement, can be as narrow as 16 feet.

Yield-Flow Streets and Roads

Design low-volume thoroughfares for yield flow.

Shelby County, AL: At Mt. Laurel, narrow lane widths
and on-street parking create a yield condition.

Older American neighborhoods reveal a third set of very small thoroughfares that still work well for drivers. As described in the AASHTO *Green Book*, a yield-flow (or queuing) street contains a single 12-foot-wide moving lane that handles traffic in both directions. As cars are less than 6 feet wide, when two meet, one pulls over slightly into a gap in the parking lane. Parking lanes are unmarked, but add 7 feet to the roadbed; therefore, a yield-flow street is typically either 19 or 26 feet wide, depending on whether it has parking on one side or both sides. Yield-flow roads, lacking the containment of raised curbs, may be less than 12 feet wide, with any parking alongside the pavement. Used judiciously in low-density areas, these thoroughfares are naturally traffic-calmed, making speed bumps unnecessary. While narrow streets can slow emergency vehicles, this impact must be considered in the context of greater overall safety. One study, in Longmont, Colorado, found that the number of lives endangered by slower emergency response was statistically insignificant compared to the injuries avoided through slower driving speeds.

8.12 Rear Alleys and Lanes

Provide rear alleys and lanes to allow walkable frontages.

Williamsburg, VA: A rear lane at New Town accommodates garage access, entrances to ancillary units, trash pickup, mail delivery, utility meters, and even construction equipment.

In widespread use in the early twentieth century, lanes and alleys have reemerged as a means of handling the growing parking and servicing demands of dense urbanism. These thoroughfares run down the center of their blocks to provide discreet access to service areas and garages. Alleys are located in urban and commercial areas and are paved from edge to edge, while lanes belong in more residential areas and consist of a narrow pavement, typically 10 feet wide, flanked by groundcover. In less urban conditions, lanes can be unpaved, with gravel or another permeable surface to recycle stormwater. Both alleys and lanes generally require a right-of-way width of 24 feet. For large cars to turn easily into garages, opposing garage faces should be kept about 30 feet apart. In addition to concealing parking, alleys provide a place for transformers, communications boxes, meters, and the other utilities that blight the streetscape with their ever-growing size. In most new towns, the wet utilities (water and sewer) run in the front street, while cable utilities are placed in the rear alleys and lanes.

Passages and Paths

Provide pedestrian thoroughfares where appropriate.

Celebration, FL: A pedestrian passage connects the main street to parking lots hidden in the interior of a block.

Not all thoroughfares carry automobiles. Just as separate bikeways should be provided where necessary to complete a regional bicycle network, passages and paths can be used to make a pedestrian network more robust. Passages are found in urban areas and tend to be 10 to 20 feet wide. They connect midblock parking lots to main-street frontages. Passages should be lined with shop windows, which add to their appeal and provide merchandising opportunities. Paths are more rural than passages and are used most often in squares and parks. They tend to be 4 to 6 feet wide and may have a permeable surface such as gravel. Paths also provide midblock cut-throughs in residential neighborhoods where blocks are too long to provide an efficient pedestrian network. Generally, block faces longer than 600 feet should be penetrated near their center by a pedestrian passage or path.

The Street

Streets are not just for moving cars; their design must also support their role as public spaces. In addition to vehicular lanes, they must include sidewalks, trees, curbs, lighting, and other elements that collectively constitute the public streetscape. These deserve serious design attention, as they all contribute to the success of a place. Rather than establish a single standard, municipalities should require a full range of regionally appropriate streetscapes that correspond to the transect. Streetscape elements should vary from the urban center to the rural edge. Common errors to be avoided include excessive lighting, unnecessarily fancy materials, sidewalk obstructions, and improperly located utility equipment. Materials that improve stormwater infiltration should be specified wherever appropriate.

9.1 Sidewalks

Provide proper sidewalks along all urban thoroughfares.

Beverly Hills, CA: In the Business Triangle, streetscape improvements created a sidewalk of ideal dimension for retail use.

With the exception of rural roads and highways, all thoroughfares should include a place to walk. In more urban areas, sidewalks should be at least 10 feet wide. On active retail streets, a 15- to 25-foot width from building to curb is not excessive, particularly if outdoor dining is a possibility. In more suburban areas, a standard sidewalk width of 5 feet allows two people to walk abreast, but wider sidewalks are appropriate for more sociable promenades along boulevards or public spaces. Narrower sidewalks are justified in rural situations; indeed, it is possible to provide a sidewalk or path on only one side of a country road. Yield-flow thoroughfares may not need them at all, as people tend to walk in the middle of the street even if sidewalks are provided. Similarly, separate sidewalks are not provided within *Woonerfs*, a Dutch concept in which cars, pedestrians, plantings, benches, and even play areas all share a thoroughly traffic-calmed pavement.

Street Trees

Provide tree cover along thoroughfares.

The all-American street: a bicyclist enjoys the sheltering canopy of mature street trees.

Street trees protect pedestrians, slow down drivers, and provide a sense of enclosure to the street space, while also reducing heat island effects and absorbing stormwater and airborne pollutants. They also increase real estate values dramatically. The proper placement, alignment, and species of trees depends on a street's location along the rural-to-urban transect. In more urban areas, each street should be fully lined by trees of a consistent species, with different streets receiving different species to limit the impacts of blight. To create canopies, trees should be spaced at a distance equal to the mature crown width. They should be placed toward the curb, typically in individual planters, and should be tall enough at maturity so that the canopy is above shop windows and awnings. In less urban areas, trees should be located between the roadway and the sidewalk in a continuous planter, from 5 to 15 feet wide. In rural areas, trees may be grouped in picturesque clusters of diverse stock at varied distance from the roadway, similar to a natural arrangement. In all locations, shade trees are preferable to decorative trees such as palms, but the latter can be justified in mild climates or where the street space is too narrow for canopies.

Curbs and Swales

Provide the appropriate range of stormwater systems.

Portland, OR: Curbside rain gardens provide an attractive
and ecologically responsible streetscape.

As with sidewalks and trees, the treatment of the pavement depends
on its location along the rural-to-urban transect. The main difference
between an urban street and a rural road is the presence of a curb.
In the city, stormwater drains via curb and gutter and is taken away by
underground pipes. In the country, water filters into the ground through
open swales. An intermediate solution developed in the northwest is
the green street, which provides stormwater treatment in the form of
urban rain gardens. A community with both urban and rural areas will
take advantage of all three systems as appropriate. Where a fairly urban
neighborhood meets a natural edge, the recommended thoroughfare
type is a drive—half street, half road—which has a curb on one side
and a swale on the other. Public works departments that have a one-
size-fits-all solution must proactively expand their technical repertoire of
stormwater management tools.

Streetlights

Provide streetlights appropriate to the location.

Ann Arbor, MI: The first city with an all-LED lit downtown will annually save over $100,000 in energy costs and reduce CO_2 emissions by 267 tons.

While tall and powerful yellow lights are the cheapest way to provide nighttime illumination, they create an inhuman environment that discourages pedestrian presence and thus inadvertently enables crime. The safest urban environments are those which attract pedestrians with flattering full-spectrum, low-watt lamps on short poles. The light standard most pleasing to the eye is no greater than 150 watts and less than 15 feet tall. Lighting levels should be achieved by increasing the number of lights, not their wattage or height. This costs more, but avoids the scorched-earth atmosphere of a big-box parking lot. Rather than be uniform everywhere, lighting levels should respond to location along the rural-to-urban transect. In urban centers and in retail areas, streetlights should be frequent—approximately 30 feet on center—in support of nighttime activity. In suburban residential areas, lights can be limited to intersections only. At rural edges, they can be eliminated entirely. The appearance of the light fixtures themselves should correspond to the transect; the more rural the locale, the more rustic they should be. To this end, public works departments must adopt a range of fixtures. Streetlights should also serve as mountings for street signs, to avoid the clutter and waste of additional poles.

9.5 Pavement Materials

Keep surfaces simple and, where possible, pervious.

Alys Beach, FL: An installation of pavers provides an attractive way to infiltrate stormwater runoff on lightly traveled thoroughfares.

The success of a street as a pedestrian environment depends more on its spatial qualities than on its materials. Funds spent on expensive surfaces, elaborate light standards, and decorative trash receptacles are usually better used elsewhere—on street trees, for example. Indeed, some retail consultants believe that fancy streetscape details distract shoppers from the store windows. The best details are usually those with an established track record, and those which are in open stock to ease maintenance and replacement. However, there are some new streetscape materials such as pervious concrete that promise superior stormwater performance; these may be applied as appropriate across the rural-to-urban transect. On the rural edge, sidewalks and pedestrian paths as well as rear lanes may be surfaced in gravel or limestone screenings that allow percolation. In urban areas, because trees grow better where water penetrates to the roots over a large area, sidewalks should have a permeable brick or cobblestone strip between planters. In suburban areas, continuous tree planters provide opportunities for rain gardens and swales.

9.6 Sidewalk Obstructions

Leave clear the path of pedestrians.

Miami, FL: Signs, light poles, trees, and planters make an obstacle course out of this narrow sidewalk.

To minimize pedestrian inconvenience, all sidewalks must provide minimum clear zones for walking. This mandate is particularly important in retail environments. To function optimally, commercial sidewalks should be organized into four zones: a curb zone, a furnishing zone, a walking zone, and a frontage zone. The zone nearest the curb should provide minimum clearance for vehicle doors to open; 18 inches is sufficient. Next, the furnishing zone keeps trees, streetlights, mailboxes, trash receptacles, and other permanent obstructions from impeding pedestrian flow in the walking zone next to it, which is thereby kept clear. The furnishing zone corresponds to the planter strip described in Point 9.5. On the other side of the walking zone is the frontage zone, along the building face. This is the place for temporary obstructions such as sidewalk dining and merchandise displays, which are ideally located under awnings. Outdoor dining should not be allowed to push pedestrians too far from adjacent shop windows. When this must happen, the solution is to locate a second clear walking zone against the frontage. Benches are one obstruction that works best against building fronts, as people are most comfortably seated facing out, without activity behind them.

9.7 Utility Placement

Locate utility equipment out of sight.

Miami Beach, FL: Brightly painted or not, exposed
utilities mar an otherwise dignified public realm.

Much of the utility equipment necessary for servicing modern urbanism
is very bulky and unattractive, and thus detrimental to street life.
Transformers, lift stations, utility meters, cable TV boxes, and other such
machinery should not be located in the frontage streetscape. Rear alleys
and midblock parking lots offer an opportunity to place this equipment
out of the pedestrian's way and out of sight. When no such "backstage"
areas are available, this equipment should be grouped systematically
and ideally shielded by a structure that mitigates its visual blight.

The Street

The public realm is shaped by the private buildings alongside, whose location and configuration contribute to its safety, spatial definition, functionality, and visual interest. To create an inviting public realm, private buildings should be situated to comfortably enclose the street space, with fronts aligned relatively closely. These fronts should have properly sized porches, stoops, terraces, balconies, and other semipublic attachments that lend activity to the street. The shape of the street space is related to the building massing: taller buildings are best against larger public spaces. The buildings' disposition on their lots should also correspond to the rural-to-urban transect, with the shallowest setbacks and biggest buildings in the most urban areas. However urban the location, skyscrapers are questionable in all but the densest cities, as they can absorb too much development potential on a single site. All buildings, large or small, should provide natural surveillance by placing doors and windows directly facing the street. Shops, to be successful, should access the sidewalk directly and incorporate up-to-date management practices.

10.1 Street Walls

Enclose street spaces with building fronts.

Gaithersburg, MD: Live-work buildings
shape a public green in Kentlands.

Humans share with all animals the twin desires for prospect and refuge.
Prospect explains the pleasure of views, while *refuge* explains the preference for well-defined spaces. For this reason most streets, squares,
and other public spaces should be designed as "outdoor living rooms,"
providing a comfortable sense of enclosure. Where gaps in the street
wall cannot be avoided, they should be bridged with attractive walls or
greenery. And, just as good rooms have simple shapes, comfortable
streets are lined by relatively flat building fronts. If facades are too artic-
ulated or silhouettes too complex, they are not as effective at shaping
the public space. In addition, simpler building fronts and rooflines cost
less, freeing funds to be more effectively spent on better materials and
workmanship.

10.2 Short Setbacks

In urban areas, place buildings closer to the street.

Denver, CO:
New houses in
Stapleton provide a firm
edge to the street.

When spaces become too large, they lose their sense of enclosure. To better define the public realm, private buildings should be placed relatively close to the street—exactly how close depends on the street's location along the rural-to-urban transect. In the urban core, buildings may sit directly beside the sidewalk. In a neighborhood center, residential setbacks might average 5 feet, which is ideal for the stoops of rowhouses and small apartment buildings. On typical residential streets, freestanding houses may sit between 10 and 25 feet from the property line. At a rural neighborhood edge, deeper front yards are appropriate. These distances should be controlled not by conventional minimum setback lines, but by "build-to" lines that designate the precise location of the façade. Otherwise, individual buildings can erode the street wall by pulling back too far. The best town plans, such as John Nolen's from the 1920s, use varied build-to lines to creatively shape the public spaces.

10.3 Building Attachments

Encourage sociable semi-public building elements.

Mount Pleasant, SC: The front and side porches
of I'On add interest to a residential street.

Private buildings shape the public realm spatially, but they must also provide it with interest and activity. This is accomplished by adding those habitable semipublic attachments such as porches, stoops, bay windows, and balconies that create opportunities for socialization. To motivate builders to include them, these attachments should be allowed to encroach within the setback zones, where they constitute an area bonus to the building. Commercial awnings and arcades are also beneficial, as they provide shelter for shoppers and expand the perceived threshold of the store. These should be placed over the public sidewalk, with easements granted where necessary. Codes must usually be modified to allow a true arcade, which places habitable space above the public right-of-way.

10.4 Building Heights

Set building heights in accordance with the transect.

Dallas, TX: The Gables West Village places four floors of apartments above shops along a trolley line.

Just as short setbacks create a better-enclosed street space, so do taller buildings. One-story structures fail to give a strong edge to the street. Where upper floors are not possible, stores should provide tall ceilings and parapets approaching 20 feet in height. One-story houses are appropriate toward the rural edge, but are not recommended elsewhere. Buildings with a partial second story should be designed with the upstairs area at the front, to better hold the street edge. Building heights should respond to the rural-to-urban transect: generally, buildings in more urban areas should be three stories or more and buildings in more rural areas should be two stories or less. Heights should also respond to location, with taller buildings placed at block corners and on larger public spaces. The often contradictory concerns of spatial definition and sunlight access must be simultaneously considered and carefully balanced.

Skyscrapers

Limit highrises to urban areas well served by transit.

Miami, FL: The city is rewriting its zoning code to avoid this sort of juxtaposition.

Extremely tall buildings, appropriate in metropolitan urban cores, do not belong in smaller cities. In the typical American downtown, a single highrise can absorb several years' worth of growth on a single site, leaving empty lots and underutilized buildings nearby. It also encourages speculation, as landowners raise their prices to correspond with the high-rise zoning. Cities that remove height restrictions in order to spur development often produce the opposite result, as each landowner holds out for the big sale. In cities without ample transit, highrises create a demand for parking that cannot be satisfied in a pedestrian-friendly manner. The best buildings for revitalizing part-empty downtowns are smaller—typically four stories or less. These allow a greater pool of developers to participate in the market, and they spread growth over a greater land area. Highrises are not a prerequisite to density. Washington, DC, has none, and New York's Greenwich Village, at five stories, contains well over 100 units per acre.

10.6 Eyes on the Street

Enliven frontages with many doors and windows.

Jersey City, NJ: New rowhouses and apartments in the Liberty Harbor neighborhood supervise the sidewalk with a variety of stoops and openings.

The key to neighborhood safety is *natural surveillance*, a term that describes how crime decreases when someone might be watching. High walls and fences, rather than provide security, block views and contribute to an environment in which misbehavior is more likely. Doors, windows, and other architectural signs of human occupancy serve as "eyes on the street." Every building should place its principal entrance directly facing the street, not on a rear parking lot. Shops with parking lots behind should not build a stage-set facade toward main street—the "front doors" must truly function. Parking structures should be wrapped with habitable space on at least the first floor, to help create a lively and supervised streetscape (Point 11.5).

Shops on the Sidewalk

Avoid shopping malls of every type.

Plano, TX: At Legacy Town Center, shops and restaurants along the sidewalk support a vital public realm.

Perhaps the most anti-pedestrian feature of contemporary retail practice is the front parking lot. For retail to attract pedestrians, the shops must open directly onto the sidewalk, with parking lots located to the rear or elsewhere. Shops with rear parking should avoid placing customer entrances directly facing those lots, as they turn the back of the building into a competing storefront. Instead, the rear parking lots should provide easy access to the street through pedestrian passages (Point 8.13). Off-street shopping arcades and urban malls are an idea whose time has passed. Many of these, such as Boston's Lafayette Place, turned their backs to the streets around them, creating dead zones that attracted crime. Finally, the practice of converting shopping streets into pedestrian malls must be considered with skepticism. The failure of more than 150 main streets pedestrianized during the 1960s and 1970s demonstrated that most stores thrive only when fronted by complete streets containing both pedestrians and slow-moving cars.

Retail Management

Design and manage shops to the highest
professional standards.

Hunstville, AL: Local stores in Providence attract business
with well-designed shopfronts and a sidewalk display.

Main streets often exist in direct competition with malls, shopping
centers, and other centrally managed retail agglomerations. To hold
their own, they must incorporate certain design and management techniques applied by the best retailers. Storefront signs, while visible to the
motorist, must be of a scale and quality that appeal to the pedestrian.
Signs should be externally lit, as translucent plastic signs and backlit
sign-awnings suggest an automotive environment. Fussiness is counterproductive; the storefront, main sign, blade sign, door, and awning
should form a simple, unified, unique design. Glass should be clear,
undivided, and extensive. Awnings should reach across the sidewalk
to give pedestrians the feeling that they have already entered the
store. Finally, leasing must be coordinated and proactive; the right mix
of shops—useful, competently run, and mutually supportive—will not
occur by chance.

The Street

Pedestrian-oriented streets are not flanked by parking lots or garage doors. Masking parking from sidewalks is one of the skills required of neighborhood planners. The first step is to implement policy acknowledging that suburban-level parking requirements undermine urbanity. Mixed-use neighborhoods require fewer parking spaces, thanks to reduced car dependency, on-street parking, and opportunities for shared parking. When inevitable, parking lots should be placed at midblock or otherwise screened from the sidewalk, and they should be laid out in a manner that allows them to be converted to other uses when land values appreciate. Parking structures must not be connected directly to the buildings they serve, since this robs the street of pedestrians. Residential garages are best placed out of sight on a rear lane, but wider-lot houses may have front driveways if the garage door is set well behind the house front.

11.1 Downtown Parking Policy

Adjust parking requirements to reduce car dependence.

Washington, DC: Thanks to Metro transit, the city has been able to lower the parking requirements for new buildings.

According to the urbanist Neal Peirce, "no great city has ever protected parking as a fundamental right." This is true, but how does a city change its parking standards without alienating drivers? The first step is to create an urban environment that encourages walking. With a better balance of uses and more walkable streets, people begin to need their cars less. This trend can then be both acknowledged and accelerated by reducing the parking requirements for new developments that meet mixed-use and pedestrian criteria. Developers should also be allowed to reduce parking requirements through the bulk purchase of prepaid transit passes for future residents. Areas well served by transit should hold developers to parking maximums rather than minimums. But in the end, it is the fate of every great urban environment to have a parking "problem." The more walkable a place becomes, the more people want to drive to it from less lively places. An emergent tourist or day-tripper parking problem is a symptom of success and should not be the catalyst of more parking.

The High Cost of Free Parking

Price parking according to its value.

Ann Arbor, MI: One of the first cities in America to install parking meters, Ann Arbor now uses a citywide pricing system to distribute parking.

Of course there is never enough parking. If pizza were free, would there ever be enough pizza? Parking, like roadway capacity, is what economists refer to as a *free good*. Most people who use it do not pay its full cost, and as a result, it is overused and subject to shortages. When parking is provided—especially on-street—it should vary in price around the clock proportionate to demand. Accurately monitored valuation will ensure that a number of spaces are always available. Donald Shoup, in *The High Cost of Free Parking*, recommends that pricing be managed by centralized meters to maintain 15 percent vacancy at all times. Shoup also advocates that developers be asked to decouple assigned parking spaces from apartments, so that nondrivers need not subsidize other people's cars. Such strategies are being used to good effect in Pasadena, California, and elsewhere. But above all, municipalities must acknowledge that investments in parking often undermine investments in transit, and they must establish their policies accordingly.

11.3 The Parking Shed

Replace site-based parking with a sector strategy.

Santa Monica, CA: America's first LEED-certified parking garage, although perhaps an oxymoron, contributes to a district-wide parking strategy.

On-site parking requirements are destructive to urban vitality. When visitors can park adjacent to buildings and enter them directly, sidewalks remain empty and shops decline. To encourage pedestrian activity, downtowns should be organized on the basis of parking sheds—walkable sectors that address their parking demand collectively. Within each shed, buildings should be allowed to satisfy their requirements with spaces located as far as a quarter-mile away. For truly compelling destinations, that distance can be farther: Denver's 50,000-seat Coors Field required the construction of only 4600 new parking spaces, as planners counted on the 44,000 existing spaces within a 15-minute walk. Such parking is ideally provided on-street and in midblock municipal lots and structures, where it can be shared among multiple users. Since individual property owners often lack the capacity or motivation to pursue collective parking, these strategies must be carried out by municipal government.

11.4 Neighborhood Parking

Reduce parking requirements in mixed-use neighborhoods.

Gaithersburg, MD: Much of the parking demand
in Kentlands is handled on the streets.

Suburban parking ratios (based on spaces per dwelling or spaces per 1000 square feet) are necessary in areas where everyone drives, but they also tend to create environments where no one will walk. Conversely, if one builds transit-supportive places in which walking makes sense, fewer parking spaces are needed. Mixed-use neighborhoods require less parking than conventional single-use zones for several reasons. They allow some people to live without a car, especially when good transit service is provided. Beyond that, they have a significant number of on-street spaces, which are available to complementary uses at different times, so they need not be provided twice. Given these efficiencies, mixed-use neighborhoods should not be held to suburban parking standards. Generally, commercial properties in compact, walkable locations need not provide more than three spaces per 1000 square feet; apartments need not provide more than one space for the first bedroom and one-half space for each additional bedroom. These counts include on-street parking and can be lowered considerably if a good transit system is in place.

11.5 Hiding Parking Lots

Locate parking lots out of sight.

Atlanta, GA: An interior parking lot at Glenwood Park
keeps most cars hidden from the streetscape.

There are few greater deterrents to pedestrian life than the exposed parking frontages of suburbia, which are simply too boring to walk past. Planning codes must not allow parking lots along walkable streets. Surface parking lots should be located at the centers of blocks, which may be enlarged for this purpose, so that they are masked by habitable buildings. Multistory parking structures should be similarly located, but may also be placed along street edges if they have habitable space at street level. Many cities now require that all new parking structures include ground-floor retail space. Ideally, upper stories should also be hidden behind shallow apartments. At the very least, garage facades should be detailed to resemble a habitable building. In communities blighted by exposed parking lots, shallow, inexpensive, and temporary "lot liner" buildings should be considered as a retrofit. These either wrap an existing parking structure or sit atop garages containing the outer row of a surface lot. When no other solution is available, an attractive wall or hedge can be built along the sidewalk frontage—but this should be considered a last resort.

11.6 Parking Lot Quality

Design parking lots for human use no less than for cars.

Port St. Joe, FL: A parking lot at WindMark Beach
uses gravel for superior stormwater management.

Even though they can undermine street life, parking areas are still public spaces and should be detailed as such. As habitable places, parking lots benefit greatly from trees planted close enough that their crowns will touch and form a canopy at maturity. It is a good strategy to interrupt parking periodically with pedestrian paths that lead toward a destination; these can be placed between car fronts or across parking lanes. Planters should be curbless, so that they serve a stormwater infiltration function. Many parking lots do not receive enough sustained use to require an asphalt surface, particularly overflow lots or those designed for sporadic demand. Lots serving churches, sports fields, and other part-time uses can be made of turf, limestone screenings, gravel, or another permeable surface.

11.7 Parking Conversion

Design parking to transition to more productive uses.

Kendall, FL: A new mixed-use, transit-oriented downtown rises in the place of mall parking lots.

Both structured and surface parking lots should be designed so that they can eventually be converted to a more intense urbanism. Sometimes a development built with surface parking becomes successful enough to warrant densification. If designed for urban succession, these lots can become sites for new buildings and parking structures without disrupting the remaining buildings. This approach requires that they be planned as a framework of traditional city blocks. Otherwise, oddly shaped parcels and misplaced utilities can make conversion difficult and expensive. Similarly, projects with parking structures may eventually be able to reduce their parking needs by improving transit. If the parking structures are designed with flat decks, rather than conventional sloped decks, they can be transformed into commercial or residential lofts. Both of these strategies cost little more than the effort of planning ahead.

11.8 Parking Lot Access

Design parking lots to maximize sidewalk activity.

Miami Beach, FL: The popular "Chia Pet" garage delivers patrons to a sidewalk lined with storefronts.

Many office buildings, stadiums, and convention centers fail to add life to their neighborhoods because they are inadvertently designed as precincts. In these developments, elevators, hallways, and bridges connect parking directly into the buildings they serve. If they are to contribute positively to pedestrian life, structured parking garages should direct patrons directly onto a sidewalk from which they can access their destinations. This technique of separating origins and destinations should be explicitly pursued: just as a mall separates its anchor stores to benefit the small shops in between, so can planners arrange parking anchors to support businesses. Ideally, parking structures should be located not directly alongside the buildings they serve but a short walk away, so that pedestrians pass by shops and restaurants every day. The same applies to parking at transit stations. As long as the walk is designed to be pleasant, few will find cause to complain.

11.9 Rear-Access Parking

Provide narrow-lot houses with rear lanes.

Shelby County, AL: Rear lanes at Mt. Laurel provide access to garages so that narrow-lot homes don't become "snout houses."

As described in Point 10.6, neighborhood security depends on the presence of eyes on the street. Doors, windows, porches, balconies, and other signs of human habitation help to make a street safe and walkable. However, achieving such building frontages is very difficult where narrow-lot houses are accessed by front driveways. When houses with 22-foot-wide garages are placed on 40-foot-wide lots, the outcome is inevitably a sidewalk diced by driveways and a streetscape dominated by garage doors. Portland, Oregon, has outlawed these "snout houses," citing their contribution to an antisocial environment. But insisting on wider home lots adds to housing costs and wastes land, and tandem garages—where one car parks behind the other—are unpopular. The most effective solution is to build rear lanes or alleys, which relegate garages to the back. When so equipped, even a four-car house can present a decent facade to the street. Rear lanes or alleys should serve every house lot less than 70 feet wide. Commercial properties and apartment houses, with their greater parking and servicing demands, need alleys even more.

Front Garage Setback

For lots without alleys, set garages well behind the house front.

Montgomery, AL: Placed toward the rear of its lot, this garage at The Preserve does not detract from the appearance of the house it serves.

Absent rear alleys, front driveways are inevitable. But there are several ways to limit parking's negative impact on the streetscape. One solution is to rotate the garage 90 degrees to create a front parking court, which takes the garage doors off the street. If the garage cannot be rotated, it should be set back a minimum of 20 feet behind the front of the house, shielding it from oblique views. This also addresses the problem that most people do not park in their garages. When the garage is recessed behind the facade, cars left in the driveway are tucked alongside the house and do not mar the streetscape. Another solution, found in older neighborhoods, places a separate garage at the rear of the lot, with a long driveway running alongside the house. This design is ideal if the driveway is nicely surfaced to serve as a terrace or play area.

The Building

The Building

Smart growth codes describe buildings not in terms of their use or simple statistical measures, but in terms of their form. These are known as form-based codes. In these codes, structures are shaped and situated in correspondence to familiar physical criteria. Within this manual, the resulting building types are described as mid-rises and highrises, commercial lofts, apartment houses, live/work buildings, rowhouses, cottages, and large houses. This list should be adapted to reflect local variations and supplemented by regional types such as courtyard and sideyard houses. One further building type—the ancillary dwelling—should be legalized universally to allow affordable rentals in single-family neighborhoods.

Form-Based Codes

Focus zoning codes on intended building types.

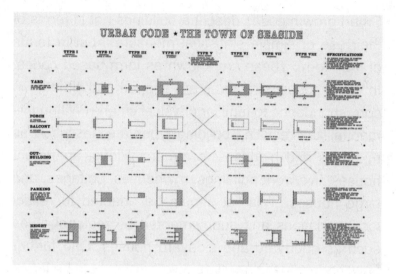

Seaside, FL, was developed with a code that references specific
building types rather than statistical requirements.

Most zoning codes control buildings by means of setbacks, lot coverage,
and floor-area ratio (FAR). These metrics bear a very loose relationship to the physical form of a building and how it meets the street. A
FAR of 1.0 may produce an attractive rowhouse with a stoop, but it may
also produce a six-pack apartment building on stilts hovering over a
parking lot. Due to the unpredictable outcome of conventional codes,
investors and buyers avoid older places that offer no guarantee as to
what sort of structure might emerge next door. They will opt instead for
the assurance of a new subdivision or office park, with its association
rules. One solution is to replace existing statistical codes with form-
based codes, which regulate buildings by controlling their configuration
and disposition on their lot. The most typical building types to be induced
by such codes are described in the pages ahead. Most neighborhoods
should contain a multiplicity of these types, selected and modified in
accordance with regional climate and culture, and distributed according
to a regulating plan based on the rural-to-urban transect.

12.2 Mid-rises and Highrises

Provide bigger buildings in the appropriate locations.

Washington, DC: A seven-story mixed-use building provides density appropriate to a Metro station.

In truly urban locations, large buildings are justified. As discussed in Point 10.5, even very tall structures may be appropriate where buildable land is scarce. In most cases, the size limitation is the parking requirement. For this reason, tall buildings make most sense in areas well served by transit. Tall buildings face the challenge of creating a streetscape that is defined spatially but not cast in shadow. As demonstrated on the Avenue of the Americas in New York City—Tom Wolfe's "Rue de Regret"—skyscrapers set back from the street with plazas fail to create a first-rate public realm. The most dependably urban tall buildings place a narrow tower atop a broad base that fills the lot to its boundaries. This is the exceedingly successful practice in Vancouver. While developers will clamor for bigger floor plates, thick towers make an oppressive and dark streetscape; slim ones yield light, airy streets as well as more pleasant accommodations within.

12.3 Commercial Lofts

Provide lofts in the appropriate locations.

South Pasadena, CA: The Mission Meridian Lofts are occupied around the clock.

The *commercial loft* is a very flexible and truly urban building type. It consists of a commercial ground floor topped by one or several stories of dwellings or workspace. It sits right up against the sidewalk, with any parking located at the rear. Lofts are found in many downtowns, but also in neighborhood centers, where they are a preferred alternative to the one-story shops that lack the height to provide an effective spatial edge to a main street. Municipalities should encourage this upstairs space for many reasons: the land is already paid for by the first-floor commercial tenant, so housing or offices can be provided for the cost of construction alone; on-street parking is often underused in the evenings and thus available to the dwellings; and apartments above shops provide an essential 24-hour supervision to the street. Affordable housing and business-incubator organizations should consider working with retail developers to encourage lofts. Municipalities need to review their building codes in order to root out unwarranted impediments to mixed-use construction, such as inapplicable fire safety requirements intended for manufacturing use.

Apartment Houses

Provide apartment houses in the appropriate locations.

Beaufort County, SC: Apartments at Habersham are provided
discreetly within a neighborhood primarily of houses.

Apartment houses are distinguished from conventional apartment
complexes by consisting of buildings located alongside streets rather
than within a sea of parking. In this configuration; the inhabitants
participate in the neighborhood rather than damaging property values
by creating a socioeconomic monoculture. One particular variation,
the *apartment villa*, is designed to fit comfortably among single-family
houses. It is the size of a large house, two to three stories tall, and
stands free on a lot about 75 feet wide. It typically holds two apartments
per floor, flanking a central stair hall. A parking lot hidden at the rear is
supplemented by on-street parking. Some of these rear parking spaces
may be housed in back-buildings, which can include granny flats above
(Point 12.10). Back-buildings are particularly recommended at corner
lots, where they shield the parking lots from the side street. Apartment
houses are generally located toward neighborhood centers, but they are
also compatible with single-family houses.

12.5 Live/Work Buildings

Provide live/work buildings in the appropriate locations.

Gaithersburg, MD: Live/work buildings with ground-floor restaurants, shops, and offices line the main street at Kentlands.

A *live/work* building, also known as a *flexhouse*, is a single-family dwelling that contains a workplace. Recent years have witnessed the revival of a number of building types specifically designed for the productive association of dwelling and working. The most popular of these is the live/work rowhouse, a party-wall building that contains a one- or two-story dwelling atop a ground-level shop or office. These buildings are organized as conventional rowhouses are, except that the rear garage may be attached directly to the back of the workspace, with its roof serving as an outdoor living area for the residence above. This arrangement, by omitting the rear garden, satisfies any additional workplace parking requirement. Other live/work building types include the loft/studio, in which work and living space commingle. Another is a conventional house tucked behind street-fronting workspace. Live/work buildings are generally located toward neighborhood centers, where they provide an excellent transition between the commercial buildings and houses. They are also useful for retrofitting suburban residential subdivisions, where an inserted corner store can reduce car trips and provide a social center to an otherwise homogeneous community.

12.6 Rowhouses

Provide rowhouses in the appropriate locations.

Cumming, GA: Thanks to laneway garages, these rowhouses at Vickery present an attractive face to the street.

Rowhouses, also called townhouses, are party-wall houses placed on narrow lots, typically 16 to 30 feet wide. Interior area depends on the building height, which can be from one to four stories. Rowhouses place a garage or carport on a rear lane. The garage may be attached to the house via a narrow wing, as long as the rear garden remains large enough to receive sunlight. This garden is a key feature: it requires walls or fences on each side for privacy. The rear lane is also essential, as rowhouses with front garages destroy any prospect of pedestrian life. Rowhouses have short front setbacks—no more than 5 to 10 feet, saving area for the rear garden. They have tall front stoops, as the elevation of the main living floor adds privacy, while sometimes enabling a basement apartment. Rowhouses are generally located in the intermediate zones of the rural-to-urban transect, where they are ideal for shaping squares. A group of rowhouses may also enfront an alley, creating a residential mews. A more compact variant, the tuck-under rowhouse, attaches the garage directly to the rear of the first floor, allowing for a shallower lot.

12.7 Cottages

Provide cottages in the appropriate locations.

New Town St. Charles, MO: Bungalow courts provide
an affordable and attractive single-family living option.

Cottages, also known as bungalows, are small freestanding houses placed on narrow lots, typically 25 to 50 feet wide. They usually contain between 800 and 1500 square feet of living space. Cottages can be one or two stories tall, but a typical plan is one-and-a-half stories, with the upstairs area located within the slope of the roof. An ideal cottage for empty nesters includes a ground-floor master bedroom. A garage or parking pad sits against a rear lane, and it may include a rental or caregiver flat above. Rear lanes are essential; otherwise, the narrow lot makes a "snout house" inevitable. Side setbacks can be as shallow as 3 feet, depending on the presence of side windows and the local building code. Cottages can cluster in small pockets throughout a neighborhood. A group of cottages can surround a small green, creating a sociable bungalow court.

12.8 Large Houses

Provide large houses in the appropriate locations.

Collierville, TN: At Magnolia Square, 50-foot lots with
rear garages provide an attractive streetscape.

Large houses are freestanding buildings placed on wider lots, typically
45 to 100 feet across. They usually contain between 1500 and 3000
square feet of living space, with three to five bedrooms. These houses
can be one to three stories tall, although a typical plan is two full stories.
They are not necessarily accessed via a rear lane, a configuration that
becomes important as the lot width drops below 70 feet. A rear garage,
which may have a granny flat above, can be freestanding or attached
by a wing or breezeway. Houses without a rear lane should have their
garages set back a minimum of 20 feet behind the house front (Point
11.10). Side setbacks are usually between 5 and 10 feet. Large houses
are appropriate across the least urban zones of the built transect.

12.9 Courtyard and Sideyard Houses

Provide regional building types in the appropriate locations.

Pike Road, AL: Sideyard houses provide private porches and yards between buildings at The Waters.

Courtyard and *sideyard houses* are building types that are common to certain regions, but that can be used elsewhere if similar climatic conditions prevail. They both have the advantage of a high degree of privacy in their outdoor areas. Courtyard houses are found primarily in places settled by the Spanish in the Southwest. They are characterized by a continuous perimeter of habitable space a single room deep, surrounding a central courtyard. They can be very close to the street, focusing one or two stories of rooms inward to the court. Courtyard houses are ideal for warm, arid climates, where indoor-outdoor living and shade are desirable, but cross-ventilation is not of primary importance. Sideyard houses are found mostly in the warm, humid places of the Southeast. They sit against one of their side property lines and face the other with full-length porches. They are typically two to three stories tall and one room wide. Rooms open to the porch and present a more solid wall against the side garden of the adjacent lot. When the porches face south or west, they are ideal for summer shade and winter sun. Regional dwelling types like these, based on local climate and culture, should be encouraged in places where they have evolved over time. Doing so often requires rewriting conventional zoning codes, which envision only suburban-style setbacks.

12.10 Ancillary Dwellings

Provide backyard apartments in the appropriate locations.

Beaufort County, SC: A granny flat atop an outbuilding adds density and affordability to a single-family house at Habersham.

Several of the previous building types mention the possibility of *ancillary dwellings*. The garage apartment, or granny flat, is a residential unit placed in the backyard of a principal dwelling as a separate outbuilding or atop a garage. Ancillary dwellings add affordable housing inconspicuously to single-family housing areas. They were once a staple of many older communities, where their presence provided socioeconomic diversity as well as quarters for extended families. These come with a built-in symbiotic support mechanism, since the landlord in the principal dwelling often watches over the well-being and behavior of the tenant. The rental payments help to cover the mortgage on the main house, making it more affordable. Despite all their advantages, ancillary dwellings are prohibited by conventional codes, which fear overcrowding, when the only real challenge is where to put the additional parking. This is best handled on a small paved pad off the rear lane, beside the garage.

The Building

At the scale of the individual structure, smart growth requires green building. Green buildings are oriented and designed to optimize solar access, and provide operable windows. They minimize heat islands by using light-colored materials and by landscaping, particularly with shade trees. In dryer climates, they substitute xeriscape for conventional lawns to save water. They conserve energy and other limited resources through efficient design and the use of sustainable building products. They promote easy evolution and repair by using open-stock materials and simple construction details, and they limit construction waste. Finally, green buildings ensure healthy indoor air quality. The LEED standards for building construction provide one of several well-established measures for rating green design.

Natural Light and Ventilation

Provide shallow floor plates and operable windows.

Cambridge, MA: A skylit courtyard and naturally ventilated glazing improve workplace comfort at the new Genzyme headquarters.

Many buildings are designed with overly large floor plates and permanently sealed windows. While initially cheaper, this approach generates greater long-term costs. Deep buildings lack sufficient natural illumination, requiring more energy-hungry lighting. These lights generate so much heat that some buildings require continuous air conditioning, even in winter. This practice threatens to make buildings uninhabitable during the peak-hour power outages that their own demand exacerbates. Meanwhile, workers feel cut off from nature and become less productive than their colleagues in sunny, airy workplaces, so sick days increase. Some calculate this loss of productivity at 20 percent. A number of corporate studies have demonstrated that the long-term costs of bulky, sealed buildings far outweigh their short-term construction savings. German building law requires daylight and operable windows in all offices.

Solar Orientation

Design buildings with the sun in mind.

Prairie Grove, IL: The Smith Residence includes a south
elevation designed to modulate solar heat gain.

Today, most buildings are designed and sited with little thought to the sun.
North and south facades are often detailed identically, with overhangs
and porches located irrespective of orientation. This practice wastes
energy and compromises comfort. Attention paid to orientation early
in the design process will result in a building that, at no additional cost,
can save energy and is more pleasant to inhabit. A building's relation
to the sun varies with climate, and a region's vernacular architecture
will provide a guide (Point 14.1). Windows and overhangs should be
sized and located to optimize passive heating, cooling, and daylighting.
In most of North America, this means placing overhangs to the south,
which block the sun in summer but welcome it in winter, thanks to the
changing solar angle. Dark-colored exterior walls, roofs, and pavements
should be avoided in warmer climates. However, solar orientation must
not be allowed to trump urban design—community health depends more
on walkable streets than on self-heating houses—but every building can
in some way acknowledge the path of the sun.

13.3 Heat and Light

Design buildings to minimize thermal and light impacts.

Chicago, IL: A green roof atop City Hall reduces stormwater and heat island impacts. It also lowers cooling costs and provides a valued amenity.

To minimize their impact on wildlife, humans, and climate, buildings should limit solar heat reflection and electric light pollution. Local heat islands can be reduced by a variety of measures, including shade trees, vegetated trellises, light-colored (high-albedo) surfaces, underground parking, pervious pavers, roof gardens, high-reflectance/low-emissivity roofing materials, and green roof gardens. Light pollution can be reduced by specifying fixtures that allow no direct-beam illumination to leave the site, particularly upward. The Illuminating Engineering Society of North America describes a range of appropriate lighting levels. Local building departments should provide incentives for these techniques, while remaining sensitive to the varying social demands of each area of the rural-to-urban transect. It is, after all, the "bright lights" of big-city main streets that lure people out of suburbia.

Energy-Efficient Design

Specify technology that saves energy.

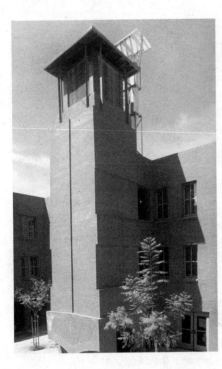

Tucson, AZ: A cooling tower channels breezes through the Colonia de La Paz Dormitory at the University of Arizona.

The energy efficiency of a building can be increased significantly for a reasonable up-front cost. A full range of building products are rated on their efficiency. These include windows, doors, interior finishes, water heaters, lighting, air handlers, and appliances. While these sometimes do cost more, the investment is recovered through lower energy bills. The same is true of walls and roofs built with superior insulation. Air conditioning systems, which are often the greatest single energy draw, should not be oversized. They should be considered secondary to ceiling fans, cross-ventilation, and, in desert climates, cooling towers. Even buildings with elevators can promote both energy conservation and occupant fitness by providing convenient and attractive stairways as an alternative. Of course, the most energy-efficient building can still have a negative overall impact if placed at the end of a long commute. When transportation costs are taken into account, the most efficient dwelling is usually the one located downtown and close to transit. A couple of bicycles in the garage may save more energy than the most efficient appliances. The energy implications of well-connected urbanism are documented in *Growing Cooler: The Evidence on Urban Development and Climate Change*, a publication by Smart Growth America.

13.5 Sustainable Building Materials

Specify construction that conserves resources.

Santa Monica, CA: The headquarters for the National Resources Defense Council was named "the greenest building in the United States."

Building materials can qualify as green if they are:

- Produced within a 500-mile radius, to minimize transportation.
- Salvaged, recycled, and/or recyclable, to minimize waste.
- Renewable, to stem the depletion of long-cycle materials (e.g., certified according to the Forest Stewardship Guidelines).
- Durable, requiring reconstruction or replacement only in the distant future.
- Produced with minimal energy use._
- Manufactured avoiding hazardous chemicals, and free of ozone-depleting CFCs and Halon gas.

In addition to wood, brick, and stone, common sustainable materials include cement/wood-fiber composite siding, cellulose insulation, laminated beams, and concrete made from fly ash. Thanks to increased demand, green alternatives are available for almost every construction product, but they will not be provided unless specified.

13.6 Buildings That Learn

Design buildings for ease of modification and repair.

Annapolis, MD: Over time, these rowhouses have been successfully transformed into shops and offices.

Buildings, like all products, should be recyclable. When we can't meet our needs by renovating existing buildings, we should create new buildings that are capable of being reshaped or expanded gracefully and at reasonable cost. While new technologies and products deserve testing, it is the commonplace materials available in open stock that are most likely to be reparable or replaceable years hence, when a building needs a spruce-up or a new wing. As discussed by Stewart Brand in *How Buildings Learn*, the smartest buildings are "durable and mutable in just measure." Simple masonry and wood shapes, with time-tested details, will last longer and accept renovations and additions better than complex configurations of high-tech materials.

13.7 On-Site Energy Generation

Harvest power according to the capability of the building.

Alys Beach, FL: Solar panels soak up the Florida sun on the roof of this house, while its white roofs minimize heat gain.

A building's potential to generate its own energy depends on its type, size, climate, and location along the rural-to-urban transect. In higher-density buildings, where rooftop area per dwelling is minimal, photovoltaic panels are less appropriate than they are on houses in the suburbs. Solar hot water systems, with their limited space demands and greater efficiency, make sense in even the most urban locations. While they are expensive, geothermal (heat-pump) heating and cooling systems become proportionately more economical in multifamily and campus applications—and they are silent, an advantage in denser housing situations. Larger institutions achieve remarkable energy savings with cogeneration at central heating and cooling facilities. A range of newer heat-exchange technologies can capture and recycle waste energy thrown off by human inhabitants and lighting systems. And at the larger scale, it is essential to reserve appropriate areas now for future wind and solar farms.

Healthy Buildings

Design buildings to have good air quality.

New York, NY: Nontoxic materials and operable windows contributed to a LEED Silver rating for the Ethical Culture Fieldston School.

Another important aspect of green building is to ensure a healthy indoor environment by:

- Specifying paints, adhesives, finishes, and flooring products with low volatile organic compounds.
- Specifying carpeting and cabinets with low formaldehyde content.
- Installing airtight ducts.
- Designing ventilation systems with a high rate of air exchange.
- Preventing moisture, radon, and soil gases from entering by air-sealing basement walls and keeping water away from foundations.
- Installing a permanent carbon dioxide monitoring system.

Because indoor air quality is a growing concern among office workers and homebuyers, a responsive design can contribute significantly to the marketability of a new building.

13.9 Yard Trees

Preserve existing trees, and plant new ones properly.

Celebration, FL: Mature yard trees add social, aesthetic, environmental, and monetary value to houses and neighborhoods.

Trees are perhaps the only element of community design that everyone can agree upon. Environmental advocates celebrate how trees support wildlife and minimize urban heat islands. Energy experts point out how they reduce heating and cooling costs. Planners and community activists call attention to their contribution to neighborhood beauty and sociability. The National Association of Home Builders verifies that house lots with mature trees sell for an average of 20 to 30 percent more than those without. Given the small cost of planting young trees, there is little excuse for not doing so. To have the best effect on interior comfort and energy consumption, deciduous trees should be placed to the south and west; evergreens are best located to the north and/or in the direction of prevailing winter winds. As attractive as they may be, palms and other decorative species are no substitute for shady canopies, which provide more palpable climatic results.

13.10 Xeriscape

Select plants that require less watering and care.

Santa Fe, NM: The native species used in Aldea are the only
responsible landscaping option in the dry Southwest.

While the lawn has become an integral part of the American image
of *home*, it is inappropriate in many climates. In areas where water is
scarce, xeriscape is the compelling alternative to thirsty and labor-inten-
sive turf. The term refers to gardens of native and locally adapted plants,
typically drought-resistant, that require little attention to flourish. With
xeriscaping, mulches are used to retain soil moisture, and drip irrigation,
if necessary, replaces sprinklers. Neighborhoods that use xeriscape do
not eliminate grass turf entirely, but they limit its use to play fields and
public squares, where it is truly necessary for human activity. Even in
these places, the grasses selected should be varieties that use less
water, such as Centipede grass in the southeast or Tall Fescue grass in
the Southwest. If explained to buyers in terms of its many advantages,
xeriscape can contribute significantly to the value of a development.

13.11 Waste Management

Use best practices to limit construction waste.

The state of Vermont is reducing construction waste through its Solid Waste Management Plan.

A 2000-square-foot house, built conventionally, generates over 4 tons of construction waste. Commercial construction can be even more profligate, and even renovations contribute dramatically to landfills. Builders who apply the three R's—reduce, reuse, recycle—to the management of construction waste will limit landfills, save energy, and slow resource depletion. They will also enjoy lower development costs. An attentive design *reduces* material use by creating buildings that correspond to the standard sizes in which materials are available, eliminating leftovers. It *reuses* construction waste by integrating demolition residue into new building and by donating unused stock to workers and nonprofit builders. And it enables future *recycling* by specifying materials such as wood and drywall that are easily reconstituted. Municipalities such as King County, Washington, offer incentives to make construction waste management easier and more economical to builders.

Green Building Standards

Use rating systems to ensure environmental performance.

Gainesville, FL: The first houses in the Brytan
neighborhood are LEED-Silver certified.

The smart growth movement is indebted to the U.S. Green Building
Council for the LEED standards. The Leadership in Energy and
Environmental Design system has become the dominant metric for
determining a building's environmental performance. Indeed, it has
become a requirement of many municipal governments for the buildings
they themselves commission—and even, in some places, for all large
building projects. San Francisco recently surpassed Washington, D.C.,
and Los Angeles in adopting the most stringent requirements so far,
requiring green certification for all residential buildings taller than 75 feet
and all commercial buildings of more than 5000 square feet. The ascen-
dancy of the LEED standard has been inspiring and useful. However, to
ensure constant improvement of all rating systems, LEED should face
competition from other green design standards, such as those available
from the Southface Institute and the Florida Green Building Coalition.

The Building

Because regional architecture has developed in response to climate and culture, the most appropriate and ecological buildings often grow out of local building traditions. The ensuing consistency of appearance is also valuable because it helps mask the potentially objectionable mix of uses and incomes present in diverse neighborhoods. For such neighborhoods to function optimally as pedestrian environments, mechanical equipment that mars the streetscape should be hidden from view. Residential privacy should be ensured through conscious building design and site layout rather than by increased distances between dwellings. Standards and policies that inadvertently cause the underutilization or demolition of historic buildings should be eradicated from local codes. Subsidized housing should be interspersed invisibly among market rate housing, but civic buildings should be visually differentiated from the common run of urban fabric.

14.1 Regional Design

Design buildings that learn from local traditions.

Fort Worth, TX: The Burlington Northern Santa Fe headquarters combines regional railroad and warehouse vernaculars.

The local building vernacular is replete with know-how regarding climate, construction, and culture. While new buildings should not be compelled to mimic their historic predecessors, designers should pay attention to local practices regarding materials and colors, roof pitches, eave lengths, window-to-wall ratios, and the socially significant relationship of buildings to their site and the street; these have usually evolved in intelligent response to local conditions. Environmentally sound contemporary design is often derived from the study of older buildings, not least because they made use of natural materials available nearby. The local building tradition also celebrates a place's cultural heritage against the tide of suburban conformity. The ubiquitous aesthetic of suburban sprawl is the result of three factors that are on the wane: the universal availability of all building materials through cheap transport, a reliance upon mechanical climate control systems, and the advent of media-driven styles of architecture, in which Orange County McMansion still reigns supreme.

14.2 **Consistency of Appearance**
Use stylistic harmony to encourage neighborhood diversity.

Montgomery, AL: The consistent architectural vocabulary at Hampstead allows for the immediate adjacency of retail, office, housing, restaurants, and even a YMCA.

The world's most beautiful places, while quite different from one another, tend to be consistent internally. Although the best urbanism contains buildings of many types and sizes, thus avoiding the "cookie cutter" effect, these buildings tend to share the same architectural language. New neighborhoods that limit their architectural vocabulary are more likely to achieve a desirable sense of place. However, there is a more compelling reason to encourage stylistic consistency: to support actual diversity. When it comes to mixing residential and commercial uses, or integrating different costs of housing, a common architectural vocabulary is a powerful tool for camouflaging distinctions that might otherwise be objectionable. A corner store will not seem out of place on a street of rowhouses if it shares the look of those rowhouses. Similarly, affordable rentals can be inserted more easily among larger houses if they do not call attention to themselves through telltale design differences. Architectural harmony helps make diversity possible.

Noxious Elements

Avoid blighting the street with unpleasant equipment.

Celebration, FL: A low wall diminishes the noxious effect of air-conditioning equipment.

Certain contemporary building practices actively undermine pedestrian-friendly street space. Although smart growth should not obsess over all the details, it must pay attention to those that make walking less appealing. Some of these consist of mechanical equipment that has been carelessly placed; antennas, air conditioning units, electrical transformers, and meters of all types should be hidden from the passerby. Dumpsters and trash cans should also be provided with off-street locations. Other items that have a negative impact on pedestrians include crude surfaces such as chain link fencing and unfinished concrete-block construction. Yet, as economic circumstances sometimes make these necessary, all plans should include secondary locations, especially alleys, where the utilitarian odds and ends can be located out of view.

Residential Privacy

Design buildings to provide private spaces.

Alys Beach, FL: Interior courtyards provide small-lot houses with entirely private outdoor areas.

Smart growth practice promotes smaller house lots, and this can increase the annoyances of living closer together. When properly designed, however, compact housing can provide a level of privacy superior to the suburban large-lot standard. For example, short front setbacks do not undermine privacy if the first floor is raised above the sidewalk. Optimally, private interiors and porches directly adjacent to the sidewalk should be raised at least 18 inches. The need for this height decreases with distance, disappearing at a setback of perhaps 20 feet. Window mullions are another useful tool for increasing interior privacy. If no outbuilding is present, privacy at a rear lane or alley requires a solid fence to enclose the yard. Small gardens, which are typically located between the house and its garage, will go unused unless protected by side privacy fences. Larger lots benefit from a rear wing or "back building" defining a sheltered courtyard. Finally, low front fences, while not essential, contribute to the streetscape by marking the public/private threshold, designating front yards as "defensible space" and encouraging well-tended gardens.

14.5 Universal Design

Design communities to serve people of all ages and agility.

Chicago, IL: The McCormick Tribune Campus Center at the Illinois Institute of Technology artfully combines a stair and wheelchair ramp.

Universal design acknowledges that most of us, at some time in our lives, will need to get wheelchairs and strollers onto sidewalks and into buildings. In practice, however, universal design can conflict with other worthwhile goals, notably historic preservation and affordable housing. The Americans with Disabilities Act (ADA) requirements can result in older buildings remaining unused—or being demolished—and new housing costing more than its residents can afford. There is also a more obscure conflict with the practice of raising residential first floors several feet above grade so that buildings can be brought closer to the sidewalk without compromising residential privacy (Point 14.4). It is impossible to choose sides among these competing interests, but one can say with confidence that no one objective should be pursued single-mindedly to the exclusion of the others. While ADA operates at the building scale, the Lifelong Communities movement implies an additional agenda at the urban scale: protecting the capacity to age in place. This opportunity exists only within mixed-use, walkable communities that allow elders to downsize without moving out, and to remain independent without having to drive to meet their daily needs.

14.6 Historic Buildings

Exempt renovations from blanket standards.

Memphis, TN: A recent renovation of the Cornerstone Building has brought residents and businesses into downtown.

Preservation is a cornerstone of smart growth. The challenge is not just to reaffirm the importance of our architectural heritage, but to actively prevent it from being carted off to the landfill. A number of current standards result in just the opposite. The most destructive of these is the requirement that renovated buildings be brought into compliance with the latest building codes. Many historic buildings, designed according to earlier regulations, cannot meet contemporary code requirements at a reasonable cost. They can continue to be inhabited indefinitely while decrepit, but any improvement results in instant noncompliance. Rather than complete money-losing renovations, owners allow the buildings to deteriorate or tear them down. This situation is directly addressed by New Jersey's Rehabilitation Subcode, which allows for more flexible and efficient solutions. Other states would do well to imitate this ordinance that, since the 1990s, has increased the number of renovations in New Jersey's five largest cities by 60 percent.

14.7 Historic Schools

Replace policies that threaten older public schools.

Cleveland, OH: The Kirk Middle School was demolished despite an assessment that its renovation would cost millions less than its replacement.

Perhaps the greatest national preservation crisis is the one facing historic neighborhood schools. These are being abandoned and replaced by new regional megafacilities on the suburban fringe. Based on calculations that include extreme requirements for playing fields, accessibility, and parking—and renovation cost comparisons that ignore new infrastructure and busing costs—school boards choose to close older buildings, despite their historic and social value. All levels of government, from federal to local, must eliminate the policy biases that favor new construction over renovation and must remove the blanket acreage minimums and other standards that make older schools obsolete.

14.8 Subsidized Housing

Mix affordable and market rate housing near services.

Boston, MA: Langham Court provides mixed-income, amenity-rich housing that fits seamlessly into the gentrified South End.

The experience of subsidized housing in the United States teaches three lessons. First, if it is to avoid stigmatization, affordable housing should not look different from market rate housing. Both its building type and its architectural syntax should correspond to the local middle-class ideal. Second, subsidized housing should not be aggregated in large numbers, since concentrations of poverty can exacerbate pathologies. Rather, it should be distributed sparsely (no more than 1 in 5) among market rate housing. This strategy will tend to avoid neighborhood blight and reinforce positive behavior. These first two objectives were endorsed by the U.S. Department of Housing and Urban Development. H.U.D.'s Mark Weiss noted, "we wanted public housing to become like *Where's Waldo?*—invisible in the urban landscape, interwoven into the wider metropolitan fabric, indistinguishable from all other types." Third, subsidized housing burdens its residents financially when it is accessible only by car and cut off from jobs, daily destinations, and social services. If it is to be truly affordable, housing must be walkable and served by transit.

14.9 Civic Buildings

Design and locate civic buildings honorably.

Milwaukee, WI: The extraordinary location and design of the city's art museum reflects Milwaukee's commitment to culture.

Civic buildings should physically embody the highest aspirations of the people and their most valued institutions. They should be placed on prominent sites that reinforce the importance of their role in the community. Since public buildings represent a collective identity, their design should set them apart from more conventional private buildings. This contrast between public and private is key to the social legibility of urbanism. Private buildings comprise the fabric of the city; their role is to provide the background of streets as places of shared use. This outcome is best achieved by incorporating a more subdued and harmonious architectural vocabulary that does not call for undue attention. In contrast, public buildings should be encouraged to take on an appropriately communicative and emphatic form.

Appendix

Useful Statements

When advancing smart growth policies or proposals in one's community, it can be helpful to introduce some clear statements describing principles and practices. Four of these follow. The first two, from Smart Growth America, define smart growth and describe how it can be achieved. The second two, from the Congress for the New Urbanism, are the organization's original *Charter* and its more recent *Canons of Architecture and Urbanism*.

What Is Smart Growth?
from Smart Growth America

We define smart growth according to its outcomes—outcomes that mirror the basic values of most Americans. Smart growth is growth that helps to achieve these six goals:

1. *Neighborhood Livability.* The central goal of any smart growth plan is the quality of the neighborhoods where we live. They should be safe, convenient, attractive, and affordable for all people. Sprawl development too often forces trade-offs between these goals. Some neighborhoods are safe but not convenient. Others are convenient but not affordable. Too many affordable neighborhoods are not safe. Careful planning can help bring all these elements together.

2. *Better Access, Less Traffic.* One of the major downfalls of sprawl is traffic. By putting jobs, homes, and other destinations far apart and requiring a car for every trip, sprawl makes everyday tasks a chore. Smart growth's emphasis on mixing land uses, clustering development, and providing multiple transportation choices helps us manage congestion, pollute less, and save energy. Those who want to drive can, but people who would rather not drive everywhere or don't own a car have other choices.

3. *Thriving Cities, Suburbs, and Towns.* Smart growth puts the needs of existing communities first. By guiding development to already built-up areas, money for investments in transportation, schools, libraries, and other public services can go to the communities where people live today. This is especially important for neighborhoods that have inadequate public services and low levels of private investment. It is also critical for preserving what makes so many places special—attractive buildings, historic districts, and cultural landmarks.

4. *Shared Benefits.* Sprawl leaves too many people behind. Divisions by income and race have allowed some areas to prosper while others languish. As basic needs such as jobs, education, and health care become less plentiful in some communities, residents have diminishing opportunities to participate in their regional economy. Smart growth enables all residents to be beneficiaries of prosperity.

5. *Lower Costs, Lower Taxes.* Sprawl costs money. Opening up green space to new development means that the cost of new schools, roads, sewer lines, and water supplies will be borne by residents throughout metro areas. Sprawl also means families have to own more cars and drive them further. This has made transportation the second highest category of household spending, just behind shelter. Smart growth helps on both fronts. Taking advantage of existing infrastructure keeps taxes down. And where convenient transportation choices enable families to rely less on driving, there's more money left over for other things, like buying a home or saving for college.

6. *Keeping Open Space Open.* By focusing development in already built-up areas, smart growth preserves rapidly vanishing natural treasures. From forests and farms to wetlands and wildlife, smart growth lets us pass on to our children the landscapes we love. Communities are demanding more parks that are conveniently located and bring recreation within reach of more people. Also, protecting natural resources will provide healthier air and cleaner drinking water.

How Is Smart Growth Achieved?
from Smart Growth America

Setting goals is easy. Attaining them is always the challenge. But after years of experience with an assortment of projects, we are beginning to see what approaches work best. Though techniques will vary across regions and community types, the ten tools listed here can form the basis for a sensible and effective smart growth plan. This list has been adopted by a variety of political and business leaders, including the National Governors' Association.

To achieve smart growth, communities should:

1. *Mix Land Uses.* New, clustered development works best if it includes a mix of stores, jobs, and homes. Single-use districts make life less convenient and require more driving.

2. *Take Advantage of Existing Community Assets.* From local parks to neighborhood schools to transit systems, public investments should focus on getting the most out of what we've already built.

3. *Create a Range of Housing Opportunities and Choices.* Not everyone wants the same thing. Communities should offer a range of options: houses, condominiums, affordable homes for low income families, and "granny flats" for empty nesters.

4. *Foster "Walkable," Close-Knit Neighborhoods.* These places offer not just the opportunity to walk—sidewalks are a necessity—but something to walk to, whether it's the corner store, the transit stop, or a school. A compact, walkable neighborhood contributes to peoples' sense of community because neighbors get to know each other, not just each other's cars.

5. *Promote Distinctive, Attractive Communities with a Strong Sense of Place, Including the Rehabilitation and Use of Historic Buildings.* In every community, there are things that make each place special, from train stations to local businesses. These should be protected and celebrated.

6. *Preserve Open Space, Farmland, Natural Beauty, and Critical Environmental Areas.* People want to stay connected to nature and are willing to take action to protect farms, waterways, ecosystems, and wildlife.

7. *Strengthen and Encourage Growth in Existing Communities.* Before we plow up more forests and farms, we should look for opportunities to grow in already built-up areas.

8. *Provide a Variety of Transportation Choices.* People can't get out of their cars unless we provide them with another way to get where they're going. More communities need safe and reliable public transportation, sidewalks, and bike paths.

9. *Make Development Decisions Predictable, Fair, and Cost-Effective.* Builders wishing to implement smart growth should face no more obstacles than those contributing to sprawl. In fact, communities may choose to provide incentives for smarter development.

10. *Encourage Citizen and Stakeholder Participation in Development Decisions.* Plans developed without strong citizen involvement don't have staying power. When people feel left out of important decisions, they won't be there to help out when tough choices have to be made.

Charter of the New Urbanism

The Congress for the New Urbanism views disinvestment in central cities, the spread of placeless sprawl, increasing separation by race and income, environmental deterioration, loss of agricultural lands and wilderness, and the erosion of society's built heritage as one interrelated community-building challenge.

We stand for the restoration of existing urban centers and towns within coherent metropolitan regions, the reconfiguration of sprawling suburbs into communities of real neighborhoods and diverse districts, the conservation of natural environments, and the preservation of our built legacy. We recognize that physical solutions by themselves will not solve social and economic problems, but neither can economic vitality, community stability, and environmental health be sustained without a coherent and supportive physical framework.

We advocate the restructuring of public policy and development practices to support the following principles: neighborhoods should be diverse in use and population; communities should be designed for the pedestrian and transit as well as the car; cities and towns should be shaped by physically defined and universally accessible public spaces and community institutions; urban places should be framed by architecture and landscape design that celebrate local history, climate, ecology, and building practice.

We represent a broad-based citizenry, composed of public and private sector leaders, community activists, and multidisciplinary professionals. We are committed to reestablishing the relationship between the art of building and the making of community, through citizen-based participatory planning and design.

We dedicate ourselves to reclaiming our homes, blocks, streets, parks, neighborhoods, districts, towns, cities, regions, and environment.

We assert the following principles to guide public policy, development practice, urban planning, and design:

The Region: Metropolis, City, and Town

1. Metropolitan regions are finite places with geographic boundaries derived from topography, watersheds, coastlines, farmlands, regional

parks, and river basins. The metropolis is made of multiple centers that are cities, towns, and villages, each with its own identifiable center and edges.

2. The metropolitan region is a fundamental economic unit of the contemporary world. Governmental cooperation, public policy, physical planning, and economic strategies must reflect this new reality.

3. The metropolis has a necessary and fragile relationship to its agrarian hinterland and natural landscapes. The relationship is environmental, economic, and cultural. Farmland and nature are as important to the metropolis as the garden is to the house.

4. Development patterns should not blur or eradicate the edges of the metropolis. Infill development within existing urban areas conserves environmental resources, economic investment, and social fabric, while reclaiming marginal and abandoned areas. Metropolitan regions should develop strategies to encourage such infill development over peripheral expansion.

5. Where appropriate, new development contiguous to urban boundaries should be organized as neighborhoods and districts, and be integrated with the existing urban pattern. Noncontiguous development should be organized as towns and villages with their own urban edges, and planned for a jobs/housing balance, not as bedroom suburbs.

6. The development and redevelopment of towns and cities should respect historical patterns, precedents, and boundaries.

7. Cities and towns should bring into proximity a broad spectrum of public and private uses to support a regional economy that benefits people of all incomes. Affordable housing should be distributed throughout the region to match job opportunities and to avoid concentrations of poverty.

8. The physical organization of the region should be supported by a framework of transportation alternatives. Transit, pedestrian, and bicycle systems should maximize access and mobility throughout the region while reducing dependence upon the automobile.

9. Revenues and resources can be shared more cooperatively among the municipalities and centers within regions to avoid destructive competition for tax base and to promote rational coordination of transportation, recreation, public services, housing, and community institutions.

The Neighborhood, the District, and the Corridor

1. The neighborhood, the district, and the corridor are the essential elements of development and redevelopment in the metropolis. They form identifiable areas that encourage citizens to take responsibility for their maintenance and evolution.

2. Neighborhoods should be compact, pedestrian-friendly, and mixed-use. Districts generally emphasize a special single use, and should follow the principles of neighborhood design when possible. Corridors are regional connectors of neighborhoods and districts; they range from boulevards and rail lines to rivers and parkways.

3. Many activities of daily living should occur within walking distance, allowing independence to those who do not drive, especially the elderly and the young. Interconnected networks of streets should be designed to encourage walking, reduce the number and length of automobile trips, and conserve energy.

4. Within neighborhoods, a broad range of housing types and price levels can bring people of diverse ages, races, and incomes into daily interaction, strengthening the personal and civic bonds essential to an authentic community.

5. Transit corridors, when properly planned and coordinated, can help organize metropolitan structure and revitalize urban centers. In contrast, highway corridors should not displace investment from existing centers.

6. Appropriate building densities and land uses should be within walking distance of transit stops, permitting public transit to become a viable alternative to the automobile.

7. Concentrations of civic, institutional, and commercial activity should be embedded in neighborhoods and districts, not isolated in remote, single-use complexes. Schools should be sized and located to enable children to walk or bicycle to them.

8. The economic health and harmonious evolution of neighborhoods, districts, and corridors can be improved through graphic urban design codes that serve as predictable guides for change.

9. A range of parks, from tot-lots and village greens to ball fields and community gardens, should be distributed within neighborhoods. Conservation areas and open lands should be used to define and connect different neighborhoods and districts.

The Block, the Street, and the Building

1. A primary task of all urban architecture and landscape design is the physical definition of streets and public spaces as places of shared use.

2. Individual architectural projects should be seamlessly linked to their surroundings. This issue transcends style.

3. The revitalization of urban places depends on safety and security. The design of streets and buildings should reinforce safe environments, but not at the expense of accessibility and openness.

4. In the contemporary metropolis, development must adequately accommodate automobiles. It should do so in ways that respect the pedestrian and the form of public space.

5. Streets and squares should be safe, comfortable, and interesting to the pedestrian. Properly configured, they encourage walking and enable neighbors to know each other and protect their communities.

6. Architecture and landscape design should grow from local climate, topography, history, and building practice.

7. Civic buildings and public gathering places require important sites to reinforce community identity and the culture of democracy. They deserve distinctive form, because their role is different from that of other buildings and places that constitute the fabric of the city.

8. All buildings should provide their inhabitants with a clear sense of location, weather, and time. Natural methods of heating and cooling can be more resource-efficient than mechanical systems.

9. Preservation and renewal of historic buildings, districts, and landscapes affirm the continuity and evolution of urban society.

Copyright 1996, Congress for the New Urbanism.

Canons of Sustainable Architecture and Urbanism
A Companion to the Charter of the New Urbanism

Global climate change and habitat destruction, accelerated by global settlement patterns of sprawl, pose significant challenges requiring a global response. The scale and extent of these problems has come into sharp focus in the decade since the execution of the *Charter of the New Urbanism*. Timely action is both essential and presents an unprecedented opportunity.

These environmental challenges complicate equitable development the world over. Holistic solutions must address poverty, health, and underdevelopment as well ecology and the environment.

Together, the transportation and building sectors account for the majority of energy and nonrenewable resource usage, making the design and planning of the totality of the built environment essential in tackling these problems.

Smart Growth, green building, and New Urbanism each have produced advances in resource and energy efficiency. Yet they alone are insufficient and are sometimes even at odds with one another in tackling this challenge. It is time for each of their specific strategies to be integrated.

The *Charter of the New Urbanism* provides a powerful and enduring set of principles for creating more sustainable neighborhoods, buildings, and regions. They have provided guidance to policy makers, planners, urban designers, and citizens seeking to address the impact of our towns and cities on the natural and human environment. Meaningful change has been achieved by simultaneously engaging urbanism, infrastructure, architecture, construction practice, and conservation in the creation of humane and engaging places that can serve as models.

Yet the profound nature of the environmental crisis calls for amplification and more detailed enrichment of the *Charter*. It is imperative for a unified design, building, and conservation culture to advance the goals of true sustainability.

As a supplement to the *Charter of the New Urbanism*, a set of operating principles is needed to provide action-oriented tools for addressing the urgent need for change in the planning, design, and building of communities. These practical principles shall be global in scope and in information sharing. In their application, actions must respond to local conditions and be continuously developed and refined over time.

We propose these Canons as time-honored operating principles for addressing the stewardship of all land and the full range of human settlement: water, food, shelter, and energy. They simultaneously engage urbanism, infrastructure, architecture, landscape design, construction practice, and resource conservation at all scales:

General

1. Human interventions in the built environment tend to be long lived and have long-term impacts. Therefore, design and financing must recognize long life and permanence rather than transience. City fabric and infrastructure must enable reuse, accommodating growth and change on the one hand and long-term use on the other.

2. The economic benefits shall be realized by investing in human settlements that both reduce future economic impacts of climate change and increase affordability. Patient investors should be rewarded by fiscal mechanisms that produce greater returns over the long term.

3. Truly sustainable design must be rooted in and evolve from adaptations to local climate, light, flora, fauna, materials, and human culture as manifest in indigenous urban, architectural, and landscape patterns.

4. Design must preserve the proximate relationships between urbanized areas and both agricultural and natural lands in order to provide for local food sources; maintain local watersheds and a clean and ready water supply; preserve clean air; allow access to local natural resources; conserve natural habitat; and guard regional biodiversity.

5. Globally, human settlements must be seen as part of the earth's ecosystem.

6. The rural-to-urban transect provides an essential framework for the organization of the natural, agricultural, and urban realms.

7. Buildings, neighborhoods, towns, and regions shall serve to maximize social interaction, economic and cultural activity, spiritual development, energy, creativity, and time, leading to a high quality of life and sustainability.

The Building and Infrastructure

1. The primary objective of the design of new buildings and the adaptive reuse of older ones is to create a culture of permanence with well-crafted, sound, inspired, and beloved structures of enduring quality. Places shall promote longevity and the stewardship of both our natural and man-made environments.

2. Architecture and landscape design derive from local climate, flora, fauna, topography, history, cultures, materials, and building practice.

3. Architectural design shall derive from local, time-honored building typologies. Building shells must be designed to be enduring parts of the public realm. Yet internal building configurations must be designed to be flexible and easily adaptable over the years.

4. The preservation and renewal of historic buildings, districts, and landscapes will save embodied energy, as well as contribute to cultural continuity.

5. Individual buildings and complexes shall both conserve and produce renewable energy wherever possible to promote economies of scale and to reduce reliance on costly fossil fuels and inefficient distribution systems.

6. Building design, configuration, and sizes must reduce energy usage and promote easy internal vertical and horizontal walkability. Approaches to energy design should include low technology, passive solutions that are in harmony with local climate to minimize unwanted heat loss and gain.

7. Renewable energy sources such as nonfood source biomass, solar, geothermal, wind, hydrogen fuel cells, and other nontoxic, nonharmful sources shall be used to reduce carbon and the production of green-house gases.

8. Water captured as precipitate, such as rainwater and that internally harvested in and around individual buildings, shall be cleaned, stored, and reused on site and allowed to percolate into local aquifers.

9. Water usage shall be minimized within structures and conserved through landscape strategies that mimic native climate, soil, and hydrology.

10. Building materials shall be locally obtained, rapidly renewable, salvaged, recycled, recyclable, and have low embodied energy. Alternatively, materials shall be chosen for their durability, exceptional longevity, and sound construction, taking advantage of thermal mass properties to reduce energy usage.

11. Building materials shall be nontoxic and noncarcinogenic with no known negative health impacts.

12. Food production of all kinds shall be encouraged in individual buildings and on their lots consistent with their setting in order to promote decentralization, self-sufficiency, and reduced transportation impacts on the environment.

The Street, Block, and Network

1. The design of streets and the entire right-of-way shall be directed at the positive shaping of the public realm in order to encourage shared pedestrian, bicycle, and vehicular use.

2. The pattern of blocks and streets shall be compact and designed in a well-connected network for easy, safe, and secure walkability. This will reduce overall vehicular usage by decreasing travel time and trip length. Design shall strive to minimize material and utility infrastructure.

3. The positive shaping of the public realm shall focus on creating thermally comfortable spaces through passive techniques such as low albedo and shading with landscape and buildings. The techniques shall be consistent with local climate.

4. The design of the streets, blocks, platting, landscape, and building typologies shall all be configured for both reduced overall energy usage and an enhanced quality of life in the public realm.

5. Roadway materials shall be nontoxic and provide for water reuse through percolation, detention, and retention. Green streets integrate sustainable drainage with the role of the street as defined public space. Their design shall maintain the importance of the building frontage and access to the sidewalk and roadway, balancing the desirability of surface drainage with the need for street connectivity and hierarchy.

6. A wide range of parking strategies (such as park-once districts, shared parking, parking structures, reduced parking requirements, minimized surface parking areas, and vehicle sharing) shall be used to constrict the supply of parking in order to induce less driving and to create more human-scaled, amenable public space.

The Neighborhood, Town, and City

1. The balance of jobs, shopping, schools, recreation, civic uses, institutions, housing, areas of food production, and natural places shall occur at the neighborhood scale, with these uses being within easy walking distances or easy access to transit.

2. Wherever possible, new development shall be sited on underutilized, poorly designed, or already developed land. Sites shall be either urban infill or urban-adjacent unless the building is rural in its program, size, scale, and character.

3. Prime and unique farmland shall be protected and conserved. In locations with little or declining growth, additional agriculture, parklands, and habitat restoration shall be promoted on already urbanized or underutilized land.

4. Neighborhoods, towns, and cities shall be as compact as possible, with a range of densities that are compatible with existing places and cultures and that hew tightly to projected growth rates and urban growth boundaries while promoting lively mixed urban places.

5. Renewable energy shall be produced at the scale of neighborhood and town as well as at the scale of the individual building in order to decentralize and reduce energy infrastructure.

6. Brownfields shall be redeveloped, utilizing clean-up methods that reduce or eliminate site contaminants and toxicity.

7. Wetlands, other bodies of water, and their natural watersheds shall be protected wherever possible, and the natural systems which promote recharge of aquifers and prevent flooding should be restored wherever possible, consistent with the rural-to-urban transect and the desirability of urban waterfronts as public spaces of extraordinary impact and character.

8. Natural places of all kinds shall be within easy walking distance or accessible by transit. Public parklands and reserves shall be protected and the creation of new ones promoted.

9. Within neighborhoods, a broad range of housing types, sizes, and price levels for a population of diverse ages, cultures, and incomes can provide for self-sufficiency and social sustainability, while promoting compact cities and regions.

10. A steady source of water and the production of a wide range of locally raised foods within an easily accessed distance establish the self-sufficiency and overall size of neighborhoods and/or small towns. Nearby rural agricultural settlements shall be promoted to preserve local traditional foods and food culture.

11. Projects shall be designed to reduce light pollution while maintaining safe pedestrian environments. Noise pollution should also be minimized.

12. The design of neighborhoods and towns shall use natural topography and shall balance cut and fill in order to minimize site disturbance and avoid the import and export of fill.

The Region

1. The finite boundaries of the region shall be determined by geographic and bioregional factors such as geology, topography, watersheds, coastlines, farmlands, habitat corridors, regional parks, and river basins.

2. Regions shall strive to be self-sustaining for food, goods and services, employment, renewable energy, and water supplies.

3. The physical organization of the region shall promote transit, pedestrian, and bicycle systems to maximize access and mobility while reducing dependence on automobiles and trucks.

4. The spatial balance of jobs and housing is enabled at the regional scale by extensive transit systems. Development shall be primarily organized around transit lines and hubs.

5. The siting of new development shall prefer already urbanized land. If undeveloped land is used, then the burden for exceptional design, demonstrable longevity, and environmental sensitivity shall be more stringent and connections to the region shall be essential.

6. Sensitive or virgin forests, native habitats, and prime farmlands shall be conserved and protected. Imperiled species and ecological communities shall be protected. Projects to regenerate and recreate additional agricultural areas and natural habitat shall be promoted.

7. Wetlands, other bodies of water and their natural watersheds, and their habitats shall be protected.

8. Development shall be avoided in locations that disrupt natural weather systems and induce heat islands, flooding, fires, or hurricanes.

Smart Growth Directory

National Organizations

Active Living by Design
(919) 843-2523
activelivingbydesign.org

American Farmland Trust
(202) 331-7300
farmland.org

American Planning Association
(312) 431-9100
planning.org

American Public Transportation
Association
(202) 496-4800
apta.com

Brookings Institute
(202) 797-6000
brookings.edu/metro.aspx

Center for Applied Transect Studies
(786) 871-2139
transect.org

Center for Neighborhood Technology
(773) 278-4800
cnt.org

Complete Streets
(202) 207-3355
completestreets.org

Congress for the New Urbanism
(312) 551-7300
cnu.org

Conservation Law Foundation
(617) 350-0990
clf.org

Environmental Justice
Research Center
(404) 880-6911
ejrc.cau.edu

Environmental Law Institute
(202) 939-3800
eli.org

Environmental Protection Agency,
Smart Growth Division
(202) 272-0167
epa.gov/livability

Form-Based Codes Institute
formbasedcodes.org

Friends of the Earth
(202) 783-7400
foe.org

Institute for Sustainable
Communities
(802) 229-2900
iscvt.org

Lincoln Institute for Land
Use Policy
(617) 661-3016
lincolninst.edu

Livable Community
Support Center
(303) 477-9985
livablecenter.org

Livable Streets Initiative
(212) 796-4220
thelivablestreets.com

Local Government Commission
(916) 448-1198
lgc.org

National Center for Smart Growth
Research and Education
(301) 405-6788
smartgrowth.umd.edu

National Center for Walking
and Biking
(973) 378-3137
bikewalk.org

National Charrette Institute
(503) 233-8486
charretteinstitute.org

National Low-Income
Housing Coalition
(202) 662-1530
nlihc.org

National Oceanic and
Atmospheric Administration
(301) 713-2458
noaa.gov

National Resources Defense Council
(212) 727-1773
nrdc.org

National Trust for Historic
Preservation
(202) 588-6000
preservationnation.org

Project for Public Spaces
(212) 620-5660
pps.org

Reconnecting America
(510) 268-8602
reconnectingamerica.org

Rodale Institute
(610) 683-1400
rodaleinstitute.org

Safe Routes to School
(919) 962-7412
saferoutesinfo.org

Seaside Institute
(850) 231-2421
theseasideinstitute.org

Sierra Club
(415) 977-5500
sierraclub.org

Sonoran Institute
(520) 290-0828
sonoran.org

Smart Growth America
(202) 207-3355
smartgrowthamerica.org

Transportation for America
(202) 955-5543
t4america.org

United States Green
Building Council
(800) 795-1747
usgbc.org

Urban Land Institute
(202) 624-7000
uli.org

WE Campaign
wecansolveit.org

World Changing
worldchanging.com

State and Regional Organizations

* Organization working in multiple states.

Alabama

Smart Coast
(251) 928-2309
smartcoast.org

Alaska

Anchorage Citizens Coalition
(907) 274-2624
accalaska.org

California

Greenbelt Alliance
(415) 543-6771
greenbelt.org

Land Watch
(831) 422-9390
landwatch.org

TransForm
(510) 740-3150
transformca.org

Urban Habitat Program
(510) 839-9510
urbanhabitat.org

Colorado

Environment Colorado
(303) 573-3871
environmentcolorado.org

Connecticut

1000 Friends of Connecticut
(860) 523-0003
1000friends-ct.org

Regional Plan Association*
(203) 356-0390
rpa.org

District of Columbia

Chesapeake Bay Foundation*
(202) 544-2232
cbf.org

Coalition for Smarter Growth*
(202) 244-4408
smartergrowth.net

Congress for the New Urbanism, Washington, D.C., Chapter
cnudc.org

Washington Smart Growth Alliance
(301) 986-5959
sgalliance.org

Florida

1000 Friends of Florida
(850) 222-6277
1000fof.org

Congress for the New Urbanism,
Florida Regional Chapter
(772) 221-4060
cnuflorida.org

Smart Growth Partnership
(954) 614-5666
smartgrowthpartnership.org

Georgia

Atlanta Neighborhood
Development Partnership
(404) 522-2637
andpi.org

Livable Communities Coalition
(404) 214-0081
livablecommunitiescoalition.org

The Georgia Conservancy
(404) 876-2900
georgiaconservancy.org

PEDS
(404) 522-3666
peds.org

Hawaii

Hawaii's Thousand Friends
(808) 262-0682
hawaiis1000friends.org

Idaho

Greater Yellowstone Coalition*
(406) 586-1593
greateryellowstone.org

Idaho Smart Growth
(208) 333-8066
idahosmartgrowth.org

Sightline Institute*
(206) 447-1880
sightline.org

Illinois

Congress for the New Urbanism
Illinois Chapter
cnuillinois.org

Metropolitan Planning Council
(312) 922-5616
metroplanning.org

Openlands Project
(312) 427-4256
openlands.org

Iowa

1000 Friends of Iowa
(515) 288-5364
1000friendsofiowa.org

Kansas

American Land Institute
(785) 331-8743
landinstitute.org

Kentucky

Bluegrass Tomorrow
(859) 277-9614
bluegrasstomorrow.org

Center for Planning Excellence
(225) 267-6300
planningexcellence.org

Smart Growth for Louisiana
(504) 944-4010
smartgrowthla.org

Maine

Grow Smart Maine
(207) 847-9275
growsmartmaine.org

Maryland

1000 Friends of Maryland
(410) 385-2910
friendsofmd.org

Coalition for Smarter Growth*
(202) 244-4408
smartergrowth.net

Piedmont Environmental Council
(540) 347-2334
http://pecva.org

Massachusetts

Congress for the New Urbanism
New England Chapter*
cnunewengland.org

Massachusetts Smart Growth
Alliance
(617) 742-9656
ma-smartgrowth.org

Michigan

Michigan Environmental Council
(313) 962-3984
mecprotects.org

Michigan Land Use Institute
(231) 941-6584
mlui.org

Michigan Suburbs Alliance
(248) 546-2380
michigansuburbsalliance.org

Transportation Riders United
(313) 963-8872
detroittransit.org

Minnesota

1000 Friends of Minnesota
(651) 312-1000
1000fom.org

Montana

Montana Smart Growth Coalition
(406) 587-7331
sonoran.org

New Jersey

New Jersey Future
(609) 393-0008
njfuture.org

Regional Plan Association*
(609) 228-7080
rpa.org

New Mexico

1000 Friends of New Mexico
(505) 848-8232
1000friends-nm.org

New York

Sustainable Long Island
(516) 873-0230
sustainableli.org

Vision Long Island
(631) 261-0242
visionlongisland.org

Regional Plan Association*
(212) 253-2727
rpa.org

Transportation Alternatives
(212) 629-8080
transalt.org

West Harlem Environmental
Action
(212) 961-1000
http://weact.org

North Carolina

North Carolina Smart Growth
Alliance
(919) 928-8700
ncsmartgrowth.org

Ohio

Greater Ohio
(614) 258-1713
greaterohio.org

Oregon

1000 Friends of Oregon
(503) 497-1000
friends.org

Sightline Institute*
(206) 447-1880
sightline.org

Pennsylvania

10,000 Friends of Pennsylvania
(215) 985-3201
10000friends.org

Pennsylvania Environmental
Council
(717) 230-8044
pecpa.org

Rhode Island

Grow Smart Rhode Island
(401) 273-5711
growsmartri.com

South Carolina

Coastal Conservation League
(843) 723-8308
coastalconservationleague.org

Upstate Forever
(864) 250-0500
upstateforever.org

Tennessee

Cumberland Region Tomorrow
(615) 986-2698
cumberlandregiontomorrow.org

Texas

Congress for the New Urbanism
North Texas Chapter
(817) 259-6653
cnuntx.org

Congress for the New Urbanism
Central Texas Chapter
(512) 633-7209
centraltexascnu.org

Envision Central Texas
(512) 916-6037
envisioncentraltexas.org

Houston Tomorrow
(713) 523-5757
houstontomorrow.org

Utah

Envision Utah
(801) 303-1450
envisionutah.org

Vermont

Smart Growth Vermont
(802) 864-6310
smartgrowthvermont.org

Vermont Natural Resources
Council
(802) 223-2328
vnrc.org

Virginia

Chesapeake Bay Foundation*
(757) 622-1964
cbf.org

Coalition for Smarter Growth*
(202) 244-4408
smartergrowth.net

Piedmont Environmental Council*
http://pecva.org
(540) 347-2334

Washington

FutureWise
(206) 343-0681
futurewise.org

Sightline Institute*
(206) 447-1880
sightline.org

Wisconsin

1000 Friends of Wisconsin
(608) 259-1000
1kfriends.org

Bicycle Federation of Wisconsin
(414) 271-9685
bfw.org

Wyoming

Greater Yellowstone Coalition*
(406) 586-1593
greateryellowstone.org

Acknowledgments

When a book is written over more than a decade, there are many people to thank. From early conceptualization through ongoing critique, final review, book design, and image selection, a group of committed smart-growthers will see their fingerprints on this manual. Many of them may not remember their participation ... it was that long ago. But we kept notes.

For their participation in this effort, we thank: Peter Allen, Geoff Anderson, Kaid Benfield, Steve Boland, Tom Brennan, Bill Browning, Faith Cable, DeWayne Carver, Patricia Chang, Bruce Chapman, Don Chen, Kenneth Dewey, Bruce Donnelly, Philip Euling, Brian Falk, Doug Farr, Steve Filmanowicz, Will Fleissig, Ray Gindroz, Ellen Greenberg, Eliza Harris, Jane Hone, Alya Husseini, Xavier Iglesias, Jolie Kaytes, Tom Low, Jane Grabowski-Miller, Laurie Milligan, Joe Molinaro, Andrew Moneyheffer, Steve Mouzon, Juan Mullerat, Leslie Pariseau, Kimberly Perette, Chad Perry, Chris Podstawski, Lori Sipes, Natasha Small, Sandy Sorlien, Paul Souza, Mort and Gayle Speck, Effie Stallsmith, Galina Tahchieva, Neil Takemoto, Dhiru Thadani, David Thurman, Harriet Tregoning, Mike Weich, Jeff Wood, Thomas Wright, and Sam Zimbabwe.

Special acknowledgment is due to Elizabeth Plater-Zyberk for her editing advice; to Dave Gibson of Draught Associates for his completion of the book design; and to Shannon Tracy for her repeated careful revisions of the manuscript during its long maturation.

For those whose assistance was somehow not recorded, with apologies we thank you.

We are also grateful to the many design firms who provided the images of their work that so comprehensively illustrate the 148 points of smart growth. Ten years ago, there were few firms who could document built examples of large smart growth projects. Now, there are many more. But for the sake of efficiency, we turned to those who, in our estimation, have been doing the most good work for the longest period of time. Which firms are responsible for which projects can be determined by turning to the Image Credits that follow.

For their contribution of images to this volume, we thank: Canin Associates, Cooper Robertson and Partners, Dover Kohl and Partners, Duany Plater-Zyberk & Company, Farr Associates, Glatting Jackson Kerchner Anglin, Goody Clancy, Hall Planning and Engineering, Looney Ricks Kiss Architects, Mouzon Design, Moule and Polyzoides Architects and Urbanists, Nelson/Nygaard Consulting Associates, Opticos Design, Reconnecting America, Torti Gallas and Partners, Urban Design Associates, and WRT-Solomon ETC.

Image Credits

The Region

1   Regional Principles
1.1   Canin Associates
1.2   Calthorpe and Associates
1.3   National Charrette Institute
1.4   Duany Plater-Zyberk & Company
1.5   Duany Plater-Zyberk & Company
1.6   Goody Clancy
1.7   Torti Gallas & Partners
1.8   Sandy Sorlien
1.9   Lee Langstaff
1.10 Faith Cable
1.11 Mike Lydon
1.12 Richard Meier & Partners
1.13 Canin Associates
1.14 Ken Dewey
1.15 Mike Lydon

2   The Regional Plan
2.1   Duany Plater-Zyberk & Company
2.2   Duany Plater-Zyberk & Company
2.3   Duany Plater-Zyberk & Company
2.4   Duany Plater-Zyberk & Company
2.5   Duany Plater-Zyberk & Company
2.6   © 2009 Alex S. MacLean / Image Courtesy of the Artist
2.7   Goody Clancy
2.8   Rosanne Bloom
2.9   Gurnek Singh
2.10 Duany Plater-Zyberk & Company

3   Regional Transportation
3.1   Moule & Polyzoides, Architects and Urbanists
3.2   Ned Ahrens, King County DOT
3.3   City and County of Denver and the Center for Transit-Oriented Development
3.4   Canin Associates
3.5   Mike Lydon
3.6   Mike Lydon
3.7   Jeff Speck
3.8   Steve Mouzon
3.9   Nelson/Nygaard Consulting Associates
3.10 Walter Kulash / Glatting Jackson Kerchner Anglin
3.11 Jeff Speck
3.12 Nelson/Nygaard Consulting Associates
3.13 David Woo
3.14 Jeff Speck

The Neighborhood

4   Natural Context
4.1   Habersham Land Company
4.2   Jeff Speck
4.3   WRT-Solomon E.T.C.
4.4   Steve Mouzon
4.5   Duany Plater-Zyberk & Company
4.6   Mike Lydon
4.7   Duany Plater-Zyberk & Company
4.8   Middleton Hills, Inc.
4.9   Steve Mouzon
4.10 Canin and Associates
4.11 Google Earth

5   Neighborhood Components
5.1   Looney Ricks Kiss Architects
5.2   Neil Takemoto
5.3   Dover Kohl and Partners
5.4   Duany Plater-Zyberk & Company
5.5   © Steve Hinds, all rights reserved
5.6   Dover Kohl and Partners
5.7   Sandy Sorlien
5.8   WRT-Solomon E.T.C.
5.9   Canin and Associates
5.10 Torti Gallas & Partners
5.11 Opticos Design, Inc.
5.12 Clark W. Day Photo-Graphics
5.13 Howard Frumkin

6   Neighborhood Structure
6.1   Regional Planning Association
6.2   Duany Plater-Zyberk & Company
6.3   Duany Plater-Zyberk & Company
6.4   Robert Benson Photography
6.5   Duany Plater-Zyberk & Company
6.6   Reconnecting America
6.7   Bob Ransford
6.8   Duany Plater-Zyberk & Company

The Street

7   Thoroughfare Network
7.1   Dover Kohl & Partners
7.2   Google Earth
7.3   Duany Plater-Zyberk & Company
7.4   Duany Plater-Zyberk & Company
7.5   Mike Lydon
7.6   Steve Mouzon
7.7   Google Earth
7.8   Duany Plater-Zyberk & Company

Index